Tim Rowland's

All Pets
Are Off

Tim Rowland's

All Pets
Are Off

A Collection of Hairy Columns

High Peaks Publishing
Boonsboro, Maryland

Tim Rowland's All Pets are Off

© 2008 Tim Rowland

Published in the United States of America by
High Peaks Publishing
www.highpeakspublishing.com

Distributed by
Half Halt Press, Inc.,
P.O. Box 67
Boonsboro, MD 21713
(301) 733-7119
www.halfhaltpress.com

Front cover photo: Hannah the English Bulldog. Back cover photo:
Opie the Bouvier des Flandres. Opie regrets losing the coin toss.

ISBN 0-9761597-2-4

Printed in the USA

Dedicated to...

Tory
Lacey
Bubba
Col. Sanders
Jake Biscuit
Hannah
Pete
Eddie
Nelson
Becky
Cappy
Bacilio
Nochero
Copperfield
Sterling
Magellan
　　and, yes, if I must, Opie...

Table of Contents

An Introduction, of Sorts

I have never gone out actively looking for a pet. I've never gone shopping for a puppy or visited the pound with the intention of bringing home a cat. Yet the pets keep coming.

In fact, no man ever needs to go pet hunting, because the women in his life usually do the job for him. He may be in a relationship with a woman who has animals, or he may be entirely on his own minding his own business when a female friend summarily decides that he "needs a cat."

Needs. Like the male species has a better chance of survival if he is ushered through life by a creature with a brain the size of a walnut.

"My" first pet was a cocker spaniel named Athena who was in actuality owned by my college roommates, Mark and Rhonda. When Athena wanted love, attention and food she went to them; when she wanted to raise the devil, she came to me. Looking back, Athena basically set the pattern.

Save for a cat named Bubba, I hesitate so say I have ever owned a pet, but I have been associated with many and they all share this common characteristic: They were and are all certifiably off their respective rockers. Maybe all pets are, I don't know. Maybe they are like children. When you see someone else's kids out in public they always seem calm, gracious and well-educated — it's only when they get back into the privacy of their own homes that they turn into Damian.

I see dogs in a park or on a mountain trail, patiently following their owners without the aid of a leash, happily wagging their tails and seemingly oblivious to a multitude of distractions going on around them. I see dogs catching Frisbees. I see dogs sitting patiently until they are told to move. I think, why can't I ever have one of those dogs?

I see cats that sleep for hours and, when they play, politely bat a stuffed mouse around the living room. I think, why can't I ever have one of those cats?

But apparently, it is not to be. And maybe that's for the best, because if I did have those smart, well-behaved animals, this book would be only a pamphlet. Safe to say, no animal I have ever come in contact with has ever let me down as a source of column material.

The cast of characters in this book — in the chronological order that they entered my life — include, but are not limited to: Tory and Lacey, two Australian shepherd mixes with good attitudes but bad manners; a black-and-white cat named Bubba, who was given to me with the assurance that it was a mild, "marshmallow kitty," but turned out to be Satan's own cat; Jake Biscuit, a Jack Russell terrier and the exception that proves the rule that Jack Russell terriers are smart; Colonel Sanders, a large, indignant and unspeakably uncoordinated Himalayan; Hannah, a sweet but self-doubting bulldog; Juliet, a noisy and opinionated Siamese; and the Bouvier des Flandres named Opie — who best as I can describe him is like Marmaduke, only not as sober.

The latter three, along with some of the larger animals that have more recently arrived in my life, are courtesy of my wife Beth, who not only has introduced me to a wide variety of critters, but taught me how to better understand them.

Not too long ago, I was sitting in my Adirondack chair and a stink bug buzzed up and lit on my shoulder. Opie, ever at my side, gave it a sniff, then looked at me and cocked his head. I looked at him and said, "Eeewwwe." He responded by bobbing and tossing his head at the joke.

Pale, I walked into the kitchen and told Beth, "I think I just had a conversation with a dog." Beth assured me that, for better or worse, I probably had. But that's not necessarily a bad thing. And lately, with Beth's help, I have learned that I do not want the dog that walks catatonically behind his owner, nor the cat that sleeps away the day.

The kind of animals I like are the ones that have been with me all the while, that is to say, uh, spirited. All my pets are indeed off; and I like it that way.

9 Lives? They Wish

I showed the story to Bubba, and I have to admit he was pretty impressed. Pretty impressed, probably, because I took time out from yelling at him for a few minutes to show him the article.

The story was about Harold and Donna Spigler of Hagerstown, who took in a stray cat.

When they took in the stray cat they were actually taking in 13 stray cats, although they didn't know it at the time, seeing as how the mom-to-be was an Army of One on the outside and a 12-pack on the inside, if you get my drift. "They just kept coming. When we took the final count we couldn't believe it," Harold said.

I'll say. One minute you have a cat; the next minute you have enough cats to stock the Hemingway house in Key West.

The Spiglers found the black cat, which they named Onyx, one afternoon in their back yard. The news story says the cat was hungry, although in my experience the word "cat" implies "hungry," and such duplication is unnecessary.

Bubba, for example, has essentially two settings: 1. Asleep. 2. Hungry. It doesn't matter whether he just ate 10 minutes ago — when I reach for the bag of cat food he leaps and lunges at it like some starving refugee desperately trying to grasp a mouthful of gruel from a bucket on the back of a UN humanitarian truck.

The instructions on the back say to give the cat a quarter cup of food twice daily. If I tried to get away with these rations Bubba would have me sitting in court next to the day care provider who locks the kids in the closet before you could say cat abuse.

Unfortunately, and not coincidentally, there is a food-energy correlation going on here, i.e., the more he eats the more he feels like tearing down a city block or two. And the more violent energy he expends the hungrier he gets and — well, you see the distressing spiral I'm in.

But back to the Spiglers. Animals are smarter than we think, I believe, and have a good sense for good people. So I don't think it was any accident Onyx picked the Spiglers. And sure enough, they've been the best of caretakers, even hand-feeding the four-odd kittens that Onyx herself doesn't have enough nozzle space to accommodate.

They knew Onyx was pregnant and they asked her how many kittens she was going to have. She mewed four times. The Spiglers said they thought Onyx was a bit misleading in her answer. But that's not so. She wasn't saying she was going to give them four kittens, she was saying she was going to give them four debate teams.

Man. How to go from two to 15 cats in less than a month. I bet they've got those "Free to a good home..." posters already printed up. A good home? Foof. Probably "free to a marginally tolerable home where cruelty isn't always the central focus of dinner table discussions" would probably serve. I'd be giving away those kittens faster than insurance companies give away calendars.

And what about names? It took me two months just to come up with "Bubba" - although some of you people insist on calling him "Bubbles," which I also find appealing for some reason.

I like the idea of naming the kittens after Supreme Court justices: There's something intriguing about a basement full of cats named Souter, Rehnquist, Ginsburg, Scalia, Kennedy, etc., but you come up three short.

If you need a matching number there are always the Apostles (true trivia tidbit: I asked my colleague Guy Fletcher to name the 12 Apostles, but he thought I said to name the 12 Opossums and implied that this time he thought I had really gone over the edge) but I don't think you want to go there.

There's something about cats and saints that are mutually exclusive.

Judge Not Lest Ye Be Scratched

This weekend offered a rare opportunity for in-depth, journalistic research at the Black Eyed Susan Cat Club's Hagerstown cat show.

I had to visit, because I'm on a mission to discover whether Bubba is really the world's most floridly psychotic cat or whether his actions are typical of the race.

Having never been to a cat show before, I didn't really know what to expect when I stepped into the Ramada Convention Center Saturday — outside of cats, of course.

And I was not disappointed. Along one wall was a long line of cats. Along the second wall was a long line of cats. Third wall, more cats. And along the fourth wall was a group of people who, I swear, were starting to look much like cats themselves. And this was just in the lobby.

I'd been warned about cat people before. In fact, I've met cat people before — usually in the cat food aisle of the supermarket. They are the ones on the brink of tears agonizing over whether little Precious prefers the taste of salmon over liver and egg. Initially I always snort at these people "It's canned cat food for heavens' sake; these pigs don't care what flavor it is, they'll scarf it down like wildfire no matter what the flavor." That's initially. By the end of the conversation though I'm always saying "Really? You've really noticed cats prefer tuna and cheese?"

By the way, does anyone know why you never see any ham-flavored cat food? Or bacon, or ribs? Do cats keep kosher?

Anyway, back at the cat show I talked with a few of the vendors, who were selling things like cat neckties, cat vests, cat earrings, personalized-while-you-wait cat greeting cards, cat mouse pads and my favorite, a greeting sign that said: "Beware Of The Dog. (And you can't trust the cat either)."

One gentleman was selling, well, I'm not sure what he was selling, except that they had what looked like a lot of tree trunks and shag carpet nailed together. He guaranteed cats would use his product because they were for "real cats."

"Some of those people here," he said, eyes narrowing, "some of these people don't know that cats are animals; they think they're human. Me, I make things for real cats. I mean cats that have been chased by a few dogs, some cats that have been caught by a few dogs and some who have even chased a few dogs. Yup, these are for real cats, cats who have lived."

I slowly backed away, and began inspecting the cats themselves. There were some very pretty cats in attendance. And some very big cats. Someone suggested I go see the Maine Coons. I said I really didn't have time for any coons, I was here to see cats. I was assured that this was a type of a cat, which they very well may be. But to me they looked more like draft horses masquerading as cats.

There were some other exotic felines that caught my attention, such as the Asgardkatt Cattery showing its Norwegian Forest Cats. They looked nice enough, but I was a bit put off by the name. I can just see a group of bundled campers circled around a mauled corpse and someone saying "Ock Bjorn, dees can ornly be der wark oof der Norwegian Forest Cats."

It wasn't until I watched the judging though, that I got an answer to my question — and herein lies the fundamental difference between dogs and cats.

At a show, dogs being judged will hold still, sit, stand, roll over, point, or do just about anything they can to please the judges.

Not here. Every last cat, while outwardly submitting to the judge, still had that homicidal look in it's eye to where you knew, given the briefest of chances, it would happily shred the judge's face to ribbons. I know that look, know it well. Bubba, it seems, is off the hook. For now.

For the Love Of Food

All the books and all the experts say a cat will only eat until it is satisfied, that it will not over-eat just because it has access to an unlimited supply of food.

Um hm.

I put this theory to the test over the weekend when I went to Blacksburg, Virginia, to visit a friend and watch the Virginia Tech-Rutgers football game.

It was a great time. Virginia Tech has as pretty a campus as you'll find anywhere, the Marching Virginians band is highly entertaining and the fans were enthusiastic and friendly to a fault.

And yet. And yet I kept getting this gnawing feeling that things were not going well at home.

Since I was only going to be away for 36 hours I hated to bother the neighbors with the chore of looking in on the world's most dangerous cat.

And, in theory, all I needed to do was put out an extra three rations of food and Bubba would conserve his meals so as to last the entire time. I didn't need to worry about the water dish, since he never drinks out of it anyway.

He prefers to perch precariously on the toilet-bowl rim, unsteadily stretch his neck down to the waterline and lap from there. I've pushed him in a couple of times to try to break the habit, but it is of no use.

So I got a big plastic bowl and began measuring out scoops of food. Curious what I was up to, Bubba came sauntering over.

Bubba has two strange habits. One, when something catches his attention, his front legs come to a stop. But somehow the neural message never makes it from the brain to his hindquarters, which will keep on walking. This makes the cat "bunch up" in the middle, sending his back skyward and a little to the left. His back legs don't stop until they bump into the forelegs and there's no where else for them to go.

The other habit is that when he is happy he will high-step without going anywhere — sort of marching place in a little dance I call the Bubbarena.

When he saw what I was up to he performed both of these habits. First and foremost, he was easily the most astonished cat on the East Coast that I was providing him with extra food. This is a case he's been arguing for months, that he is fed nowhere near enough. Rapt in my activity, his back legs bumped into his front legs uncommonly hard, and he almost went down.

Just in case, I gave him the three scoops he'd normally get, plus two more for good measure. Bubba, not believing his good fortune began to dance as never before - almost to the point that it resembled some prehistoric ritual of thanksgiving a caveman might employ prior to feasting on a particularly plump mastodon.

As I took some stuff out to the car he began to dine. When I returned he had gone through Friday's dinner and started in on Saturday's breakfast. By the time I left we was working his way into Sunday brunch.

I explained the situation to him, but little he cared. I calculate he had polished off every last scrap by the time I hit Winchester.

Which, of course, left him with nothing to eat for the next day-and-a-half and with nothing to eat he had nothing to do — except plot.

You would think the cat would have credited my account for giving him extra rations in the first place. But this is not how Bubba saw it. All that registered with him was that mealtimes were passing sans meals.

As a reaction, he did some creative rearranging of things I would have preferred be left unrearranged.

Plus, I got a massive dressing down from him when I returned. This is annoying because I was right in the way I handled things, and I know I was right, but there's no way to get the point across to a cat.

Fortunately, he's easy enough to mend relations with — just give him more food.

The Nobel Prize for Stupid

It was something on the order of trading in one brand of trouble for another.

The dogs were coming up for a visit, and while I thought it might be something of a good time, putting all three critters in a single room, others said it would be a form of animal abuse and suggested I'd best sequester the cat.

So out went Bubba to a friend's house, and in came Tory and Lacey. Teeming with intelligence, as usual. Brilliance is just oozing out of their cranial cavities. I tell you, if they had a game show for dogs this pair would have more kitchen appliances than Spicher's.

Right.

Here's how I happened to get the two idiots in the first place: Their owner's aunt was getting married and the reception was at the home. For some unfathomable reason, her mom didn't want the two dogs scurrying around beneath the bride and groom, so they got the honor of sleeping under my bed for the weekend. The dogs, I mean, not the bride and groom.

Even so, this strategy proved not to be airtight. During a brief stopover on their way here, the dogs bounded through the reception-decked home and Lacey, of course, ran under the dining room table which, of course, was spread with a long tablecloth which, of course, got snagged on Lacey's skull and followed her around the room.

Luckily there was only one breakable thing on the table at the time. Unluckily it was the custom-made Champaign glasses for the toast with "Bill and Diane Forever" etched on the side.

Forever or until Lacey got hold of them, whichever came first. And as fate would have it, it was the dog. Egads, if spilling the wine on the wedding day is bad luck, imagine the consequences of the custom-made glassware shattering into a bajillion pieces the night before. If they're still together after the cruise it will be a miracle.

So after a side trip to Annapolis to buy new glasses, I brought the dogs home. On Saturday I needed a place to take them where they couldn't break anything else, and settled on the Antietam battlefield.

I'm sure the park service frowns severely on taking a couple of mutts cross-country over the fields, but I figure we've paid for enough "buffer zone" land in recent years for us to be entitled.

Perhaps it's a testament to its preservation, but Antietam can be a very spooky place. It's way too easy to stare across a field and see a thicket of smoking rifles pointed your way.

You never can say how you would react under specific circumstances, but I don't think I could have done it. Antietam makes it seem all to real.

Then I think about all the people who fought in the world wars, Korea, Vietnam and these other spats around the globe — places that aren't even on home soil. They are better men and women than I am, every one.

But every time I get philosophical like that and lose track of things I'll invariably catch an Australian shepherd going full-bore in the small of my back. To them this is big fun, sending me sprawling among the corn stalks and Civil War ghosts.

To me it's a mixed bag. Part of the benefit, I thought, of taking the dogs to Antietam, as opposed to the towpath or one of the state parks, is that it is dry — or should have been dry.

But these dogs could find a mud puddle on Neptune.

And they always find it right before I'm ready to leave, so the car smells of dogswamp for the next 18 weeks.

After the weekend I traded Lacey and Tory in for Bubba.

It's sort of a wash. They all shed, wake me up an unbearable hour and get into things they shouldn't. But the weight ratio is 110 pounds to six.

I'll take the cat.

Giving the Vacuum What-Fur

The primary downside of owning a cat is the accumulation of fur.

OK, OK, the primary downside of owning a cat, aside from the noise, the midnight howling, the expense, the smell, the open wounds caused by sharp teeth and claws, the four-in-the-morning alarm call, the frequent sound of breaking glass, the ungratefulness, the fickleness, the property damage, the attacks on covered feet in the middle of the night, the stubbornness, and the refusal to leave anything alone, is unquestionably and without a doubt the accumulation of fur.

I notice this because it is spring-cleaning time. To say the issue is more urgent this year is a bit of an understatement.

Thanks to Bubba, everything in the place — rugs, tablecloths, napkins, bedspreads, chairs — has taken on this misty gray haze that, photographed from outer space, would probably be mistaken for a heavy, alto cumulus cloud system moving in over Hagerstown.

Take your rubber-soled foot and scuff it back and forth on the rug a couple times and you come up with a fibrous mass that looks something like a bale of rolled hay.

So it was obvious I needed some basic cleaning supplies. And when I say basic, I mean a vacuum cleaner. I also needed something to spruce up the place in the way of plants, so things would look all spring like.

I do this every year. Every year I fail. I drove out to Beaver Creek (the only time I'm allowed in the Beaver Creek area is when I plan to spend money; else wise there's always a state trooper jabbing a night-stick into the small of my back saying "keep it moving scum").

But at a nursery there I was helped by a very kind and optimistic woman who fixed me up with some herbs she said I probably couldn't kill for at least three to four weeks unless I really tried.

When I got them home the cat glanced up and you could see one word flash across his beady little eyes: "Lunch."

Buying a vacuum was a little more difficult. I walked into the department store and went to the cash machine, which is a very efficient invention in that they only charge you $2 for each $1 you take out.

But I couldn't use the ATM because standing three inches in front of it was a bespectacled, baseball-capped old goat, mouth agape, staring at this money-dispensing machine from its peak down to it's base and then back up to its peak. So intent was he on its detail, its lines, its symmetry, that at first it appeared he was thinking of having one made like it.

He looked at this machine with as much florid disbelief and unharnessed awe as a Zambian gorilla who'd chanced upon a seven-foot banana.

He wouldn't leave, so I did — across the street to a store where shopping was a truly bizarre ordeal. I found the compact vacuum I wanted all right, but you couldn't just pick up the vacuum and take it to the checkout counter. Oh no. You had to fill out a ticket and hand it to a helpful person who punched your order into a computer terminal.

Then, while you wait, you are sold an extended warranty service, which is a little like an HMO plan for vacuums, although more expensive than traditional health care. Then you fill out a credit application and wait around until you are denied, then they give you some coupons and other literature and only then can you go to the cashier where perhaps or perhaps not your purchase is teetering down a conveyor belt.

It may be a vacuum, it may be a Kiddie-B-Gone outdoor playpen, you're never really guaranteed.

I got the vacuum home all right, but was too exhausted to use it. It was still a good deal though. Because when I gun the motor a couple times it scares the living kibble out of the kitten and keeps him away from the herbs. An expensive cat deterrent, I grant you, but darn effective.

Coupons for Cats

Sad news in the papers this week. The stories say that the grocery store coupon, with more than 100 years of history behind it, may have begun the long, slow slide into oblivion.

If you have ever gouged another woman's eyes out with a hot knitting needle, and I know that you have, to get her $1-off-any-two-boxes-of-Post-cereal coupon, you understand the loss.

Because, by gosh, this is America, where we have the honor and the right, nay the obligation, to take 20 cents off a 96-ounce bag of Mrs. Paul's semi-sweet oven-ready concentrated country style pork potato drumlets.

I have changed my opinion of coupons; where I used to treat them as items of nuisance, I have grown to love and respect them. I clip coupons every Sunday morning, which is not to say that I ever get around to using them.

But it's comforting, it's sort of a trip down memory lane. You get to see all those revitalized products that you more or less assumed they stopped making years ago. Like Doan's Pills. I had no idea they were still in business. But they're alive and well, with a new carton and at 40 cents off to boot. And you know they work, because the box has a drawing of a guy holding his back and then a drawing of the same guy not holding his back.

With Bubba the remorseless eating machine in tow, I pay lots of attention to pet coupons. Bubba, by the way, is the only cat I know who purrs while he eats — actually "purr" is too kind and gentle a word for a noise that sounds more like backhoe tearing into a limestone ledge.

I like the coupon descriptions of animal food. Alpo is "highly digestible." What a concept. It's also the "best taste ever." Really? As determined by who? Do they have bald guys sitting around in moldy tuxes saying "I do say, Albert, this one much reminds me of a 1968 Alpo with its stout character and a bouquet that recalls baskets of freshly harvested horse kidneys."

Then there's something called "Deli-Cat," which, judging by its name, is either a product made for your cat or out of your cat, you can't really tell.

We have Mighty Dog: "It makes your dog a Mighty Dog." These people have never experienced my dogs. If they had they would know a mighty dog is not a good thing. They would want a cautious, reserved dog. They would name their food "Zombie Dog."

This isn't even to mention all the cat litters. My personal favorite is Scoop Away, because there is a coupon for the "Scoop Away mailing list." Is anyone else more than a little frightened over what the postman might bring if you sign up on the Scoop Away mailing list?

I also like the little visual aids that set off the coupons. The sandwiches are all very pretty. That's because they don't use real lettuce, they have perfect, shiny green and curly stunt lettuce that comes into the shoot, takes off its stole and sunglasses, posses with the baloney then gets into its limo and drives back to its mansion in Beverly Hills.

The Rubbermaid dustpan, pictured with fake dirt, is good. You need dirt in the photo so we will know it works. But it can't be messy dirt, it has to be happy dirt. So they cut strips of construction paper into brightly colored confetti and place it in the dustpan. That way we know it works, but we're not grossed out.

Rivaling this are the Harvest Burger recipe cards. I'm not entirely certain what Harvest Burger is, but the coupon is set off by a photo of a recipe file. All the cards that call for hamburger have "hamburger" scratched out and "harvest burger" written in. Thanks for the tip.

Can we live without this Americana, these works of culinary cultural art? Hard to imagine. But at least there will be fewer maimings attributable to the Sunday inserts.

Cat Doesn't Love a Parade

If you can see your breath in November, it must be Mummers' Parade night.

That and there's something called a "Woolly Bear Contest" going on. I'm not surprised that we have an actual competition to judge the biggest, hairiest and surliest woolly bear caterpillars. There's nothing else to do with them — at least until someone comes out with a cookbook. I just wish I'd known about the contest back when I was a kid growing up in Morgan County. Now there we had some woolly bears. Big? You bet. Ornery? I remember a farmer telling me he caught one of the little monsters trying to run off with one of his chickens.

When I didn't act impressed enough, he said he had even caught a couple of the old cantankerous caterpillars trying to vote.

This wasn't even close to being believable, and finally the farmer backed down from his story, saying it looked as if they were voting, but in fact they may only have been conducting exit polls for the networks.

For a while I thought about dying Bubba's white spots brown, pruning his ears and entering him as a woolly bear this year. But when I saw woolly bear judge Frank Leiter quoted as saying he took personality into account, I abandoned the experiment.

Besides, Bubba can't keep his fool mouth shut for 20 seconds, and it would be highly embarrassing if halfway through the contest a woolly bear up and meowed.

But I did let him watch the Mummers' Parade. That is, he watched it when he wasn't hiding under the bed.

The parade was still out of earshot, and Bubba had arranged himself artfully on the dining room table. He was falling into one of those luxurious, enviable cat sleeps, where the eyes slowly give way horizontally to more and more fur until they are evidenced by nothing more than two dark slits. He put his ears on standby, turning them outward slightly. His head was still erect, but it looked as if every other bone in his body had dissolved and he drifted off, looking as comfortable and serene as a southern preacher whose wife was off on holiday.

Then the band exploded to life — and with it, Bubba. His eyes bolted open and I thought his ears were going to pop straight off his head, like poison darts out of an aborigine blowgun.

Never have I seen a cat decide so instantaneously that bands were not his barrel of fish. Bubba took up residence under the bed until certain these dangerous, instrument-wielding students were not going to come up the stairs to get him and pass him triumphantly around overhead like a one-cat mosh pit.

He reappeared after a time, tail twitching, and taking full credit for scaring away this noisy brass host. It was about this time he noticed the movement, the floats, the people, the commotion, the fire trucks — all on his street corner.

Obviously all this needed to be killed.

He sat on the sill muttering shrilly, every so often wheeling his head to look at me accusingly — all I had to do was let him out and he'd personally take care of this disturbance. He was just the cat tough enough to do it; he'd give them what fur and then we'd see who was...

...but then came another band and Bubba's reborn interest in studying the southern exposure of the box springs.

I suppose if I had wanted something brave I would have gotten a pet ferret. Or a pet woolly bear. I've never seen a woolly bear run away from anything, or back down from a confrontation.

Of course that means they usually get eaten or run over by a bicycle tire. This will never happen to Bubba. He may sacrifice some pride, but he will never allow himself to be tracked down and massacred by a Washington County band student.

The Cat Box That Mops Up

You won't hear my normal sermon this autumn about Christmas decorations going up too early. That's because I already know what I want, thanks to the entirely bizarre Hammacher Schlemmer (home of the $169.95 golf ball) mail order catalog.

It's on page 58 and is advertised as the world's "only self-cleaning litter box," listing at $199.95. I'll quote straight from the text:

"A built-in microprocessor-controlled system makes this the only litter box that cleans up after your cat. Sensing when your cat has left the litter box, its electronic eye signals the sifting comb which moves through the length of the box, scooping up waste and depositing it into a PVC plastic holding cartridge."

As Bart Simpson would say, "cooool."

A cat box that has more RAM than my computer.

The little synopsis says that the cartridge's airtight container "eliminates lingering odors." I'll be honest, it's not the "lingering odor" that gets me down. It's more the "first offense," as it were. Compared to that, anything that lingers is tantamount to violets.

The serious downside to this machine is that the throw-away waste-storage canisters are two for $10. So every time you toss out the cat litter you're tossing out a fin along with it — but what else would you expect from a company whose audience is willing to pay $2,500 for an F-16 flight simulator?

So I believe I'll stick with my current kitty septic system.

And really, it's not the way Bubba (the world's most dysfunctional cat) uses his litter box that bothers me so much, it's more his attitude toward it.

While most cats consider litter to be an article of sanitation, he considers it an article of artistic expression. To begin with, he head-butts the cat box around the house to different locations as if it were a potted plant, then sits back with a critical eye to get a perspective. If he's dissatisfied with the look, he butts it off somewhere else.

Which is all well and good if only he'd put it back. But I tell you, there's no worse way to start your day than to swing your feet over the bed in the morning and have them land square in the cat box.

But it's only after he's settled on a location that things really start to get weird. That's when he rolls up his sleeves, symbolically speaking, or course, and begins to shape the litter in thoughtful crests and dells sort of like he were trying to artfully frost a cake.

Then he goes into the landscapes, the still lifes, the impressionism and the post-modern. No cat ever agonized so over where to arrange every last scoopful of clay. He'll spend half the day in the cat box and never use it for its intended purpose once.

I'll come home at night and catch him sitting there darkly brooding over some perceived artistic flaw in the topography — as eluded by the one cant or indentation which might make the mediocre into a masterpiece suitable for the Hirshhorn.

I'll wake up in the middle of the night and I'll hear him — scratching, patting, pushing, fussing, arranging.

Perhaps for Christmas he doesn't need a new cat box, he needs a potter's wheel.

But then he's never hit upon a design he's found suitable for saving. And actually this entire ritual may be less art than it is pregame ceremony.

For when he does use the box as it is to be used, it's Katie bar the door — he destroys his long-pained architecture like a wave destroys a sand castle, kicking up his hind paws with a fury that sends litter from here to Williamsport.

Temperament of an artist, I suppose.

It's like Charlie Brown always says about Snoopy. I wonder what it would be like just to have a plain-old-cat cat.

Pet Psychics Need Not Apply

No, I didn't take Bubba to the SPCA sponsored pet psychic over the weekend. Not that it wasn't tempting — if I didn't like the forecast, I could "accidentally" leave him at the shelter. Surely there's some family out there who would enjoy the feline equivalent of some Serbian war criminal.

But then it did seem to be a bit of a waste. Because if I wish to predict the cat's future I can do it. Exactly three years from today, I predict he will awaken at 6 a.m., scream for his food, take breakfast at 6:30 when I can no longer stand his howling, race around the house like a rabid greyhound, go to sleep, awake at 4:30, scream for food, take dinner at 5 when I can no longer stand his howling, race around the house like a rabid greyhound and go to sleep.

It's not as if his calendar needs to be arranged by a social secretary from the Kennedy administration.

Looking back now, I'm even more glad I didn't take the cat in for an evaluation. Because it seems the psychic Luanne Umfer was not only making predictions, she was taking depositions. She would say that an animal was lonely, or that his feelings were hurt.

In other words, this was the perfect chance for a pet to hand up an indictment against its owner. This is not the sort of opportunity Bubba deserves.

I can see myself standing there in front of everyone at the SPCA open house, sweating profusely and saying "Don't listen to him, you know how those cats lie!"

That's all I need. I already received enough grief for defending the right of a Greencastle elementary school to butcher a turkey. People said I was being mean to animals and that I should "save my venom for the County Commissioners."

But there is an animal I would like to have taken to Ms. Umfer — and that is a Winchester, Virginia-area deer I heard about recently. Apparently this critter leaped through the picture window of a stately home and proceeded to trash the interior.

Then he bounded down the stairs into the rec room. But it was bad judgment. For the homeowner was a hunter and across the basement wall was a row of mounted deer heads.

Now imagine how you would feel if you were lost in the woods and beginning to panic. You stumble down a hillside and suddenly you see, nailed to a tree, the mounted heads of the entire cast of 90210? OK, scratch that. Suppose it were the heads of a half-dozen people whom you would *not* want to see stuffed?

It would be pretty grim, wouldn't it? Well our deer felt the same way, because he instantly developed an intense interest in evacuating that particular home. Either that or he remembered a deer PTA meeting he was late for.

Whatever, he bolted up the stairs, back through the broken window, across the yard and out into the highway — where, I am not kidding, he was promptly hit and killed by a car.

I don't know whether you believe in luck or not, but this was a deer you definitely did not want picking your lottery numbers that day.

Authorities, meanwhile, said this is just another example that the deer population has gotten too thick.

So thick, in fact, that on the news Monday night was a report that Montgomery County is thinking about shooting deer with contraceptive darts so they won't reproduce.

Three questions: 1. Can they do that? 2. If they can, how come it escaped notice of Newt Gingrich when Republicans were drawing up their new Welfare-reform bill? 3. Could I have saved $32 in neutering expenses?

I might have tied some antlers to his head like the dog Max in "How the Grinch Stole Christmas" and sent him out into the woods in Montgomery County. I bet they'd have plugged him for free. Along with too many deer, the state already has an overpopulation of Bubbas.

An Assault of the Hiccups

If you have never had the occasion to watch a cat get the hiccups, you haven't lived. I'd never witnessed such an event until this weekend, when Bubba became afflicted. Either he swallowed wrong, breathed poorly or ate too fast (always a logical presumption when it comes to Bubba).

If my friend Frank (the Bubba Doc) or any other veterinarians are reading, they might want to consider patenting an inoculation that will give cats a case of the hiccups every so often, solely for the pleasure and entertainment of their owners. It's not cruel; cats owe us cat owners something for all they put us through, and I think this is a good, sound, nonpainful form of repayment.

Bubba had climbed up on the stereo speaker when he was stricken. He is a perfectly trained cat and never jumps up on anything he is not allowed to jump up on.

That's because there is nothing he is not permitted to jump up on. We came to this understanding early on. Training isn't in my cards and being trained isn't in his. He keeps his nose out of my food and I keep my nose out of his, and that's about all we ask of each other.

Anyway, he's arranged himself over the speaker in an attitude that could be comfortable only for a cat — hind legs draped off the eastern exposure, forelegs draped off the western exposure and the head hanging off the northern exposure in a contortion that for a cat suggests blissful comfort, but for a human would suggest having been hit by a bus.

Then, the first convulsion hit.

You know when a person gets the hiccups how the head might jerk a little? Or sometimes, if the case is really severe, you might see a slight twitch in the neck, or a heave in the chest, at the most?

Well, when Bubba was rocked with the first hiccup, all four legs locked straight out, his eyes bugged and he lifted a full inch off the speaker, so violent was the attack.

The beauty of this was, having apparently never had a case of hiccups in his life, Bubba had no idea what hit him. He sat up at full alert, like "What the heck was that?"

And after two minutes, he settled back down into his former pose, figuring, perhaps, he had dreamed the whole thing.

Another minute passed.

Then, he got walloped again. Again, his entire countenance became airborne and he landed back down on the woodwork with an ungracious whump.

Now, though, he was dealing with another tribulation, aside from the hiccup itself — that being me on the floor drowning in laughter, so total was his befuddlement.

He could stand the physical symptoms, but not this affront on his dignity.

And here I was, paralyzed in glee at the cost of his ego and self-respect.

Inwardly, he began to seethe.

He glared out the window, he glared at me, he glared at a plant. His thoughts turned black and he began to calculate ways in which he could get even, and what tortures he would inflict on everyone and everything responsible for this and furthermore, he .... WHAM!

A particularly powerful hiccup somersaulted him skyward and temporarily shock-therapied all those evil thoughts from his brain.

Upon landing, he suddenly remembered an errand he needed to accomplish under the bed.

This was Monday. I've seen him once or twice since, always in fleeting moments when he'll come out to grab a snack or bite a passing toe. But at night, I hear him pacing, his mind, I'm sure, bent on revenge. No cat has ever thought over a plot so thoroughly as this animal has been doing all week.

It's making me nervous. Everything indicates he is considering a profoundly stiff penalty. If you're guessing "cat" in the "kitchen" with the "lead pipe," you might have the winning hand.

My only hope is that if a cat can catch the hiccups, he also might be susceptible to amnesia.

The Flying Mouse

Being a city cat, Bubba hadn't had much experience with the outdoors, or much of a resume for killing that didn't involve arachnids. But when forest-owning friends went out of town and pegged me to housesit, I told him the time had come for him to quit squawking and start stalking.

Trouble is, his first stalk involved a resident of the house, a wizened old tailless cat named Pretzel. With a disposition like the Queen Mother, only not as cheery, Pretzel immediately responded to the advances with a few well-placed, claws-out swats that seemed to baffle Bubba — and persuaded him that other cats, not rodents, were the enemy. This perfectly suited the designs of the passive-aggressive Pretzel, who teamed up with Bubba to engage in a feline rein of terror against any and all neighborhood cats against whom Pretzel had conceived a spite over the past decade.

They were almost like the stereotypical police partners. Pretzel, reserved, cerebral and cagey; Bubba, wild, brawny and beyond stupid. Where Pretzel knew to stop at the property line, Bubba would keep on stalking, deep into enemy territory. I would watch him lurk, slow and low to the ground, continuing the pursuit until he was out of sight.

About 10 minutes later, there invariably would be a loud report (a raucously barking dog or screaming housewife, as a general thing) and the black and white streak of the cat would come tearing back into the yard, ears and tail streaming straight back like laundry during a West End tornado.

After enough of these adventures, Bubba seemed to conclude that more modest prey was in order. I tried to help him. I actually heard a mouse rooting around under some groundcover and kicked it out into the open where I bounced it on my foot like a game of rodent hackeysack, him squealing in protest.

I stepped back, foolishly assuming the cats would move in for the kill. But when I looked up, there were Bubba and Pretzel all right, but instead of fixing their attention on the escaping mouse, they were staring at me as if I were nuts to be wasting my time with this fur-encrusted squeal.

This is why women and cats get on so well — they're both so freaking hard to impress.

But the killing instinct must have engaged Bubba all at once, because Saturday morning I came out the door to fine not one, but three little mousie carci on the patio.

So we sat outside that morning, me with a book and Bubba basking in the revelries of the kill. But his thirst for blood was unquenched, because in an instant, as I watched, he spanned the yard, hunkered down, quivered all over and pounced.

Triumphant, he returned to the patio with the poor little creature wriggling in his jaws of death.

Young as he is, Bubba has a weakness for the classics and he sat down to a traditional cat game of chase and catch. He spit out the rumpled thing, gave it a bat — and watched in pure amazement as this mouse spread its tiny wings and flitted away into a tree, where he unleashed a barrage of bird profanity at the stunned cat.

Never has a carbon-based life form been more mentally uprooted than was Bubba over this Flying Mouse. He acted hurt. He looked up at me like "can they *do* that?"

So far as I know, that was his last hunt. He seems to have soured on the process. If they can't play fair, he won't play at all. Because of that, I believe he'll be happy to come back to the city — assuming he doesn't encounter any flying spiders.

Bubba Gets the Blues

Several people have mentioned recently that it has been a while since I've written anything about the cat named Bubba.

And they say this as if that is a bad thing.

I've even had some people suggest there might be some sinister circumstance behind this disappearance from print, as if I would bind and gag a cat and hide him away in the trunk of a Buick.

No, that has not happened. Although now that I think about it...

Truth is, it's not as if Bubba is a tremendously complicated cat, who lives out complicated plot lines that need weekly, or even monthly, exploration.

Faulkner he's not. His interests are basically confined to food, moving objects and moving objects that can be construed as food, such as spiders and swaying fronds on a potted palm.

To be sure, his lack of native intelligence and coordination can occasionally turn these rather simple rote disciplines into wild theatrical performances worthy of Jim Carrey on hallucinogenic mushrooms.

What starts out as a ho-hum lick on the forearm can end 30 minutes later in a sea of disheveled rugs and smashed crockery, depending on what nonexistent ghost catches his attention from the time he extends his tongue to the time it swabs his fur.

Except that lately Bubba seems to have developed an affinity for music in general and the blues in particular.

To be honest, a couple of years ago Bubba would not have had the opportunity to ever hear the blues because I never would have conceded to have such atrocities in my house.

But I am growing. I have learned that the blues are more than simply for people who, as George Carlin put it, are "just a little strange."

Last year I was excited about the Western Maryland Blues Fest (I'm trying to get them to change the name to something more catching, like Bloozeapalloza, but so far have been greeted with limited enthusiasm) because of the event and the promise of food. This year I am excited about the music.

At the risk of sounding like a message from the Ad Council and this station, this weekend's Blues Fest is bringing together a tremendous field of artists — in an unbelievably short period of time, this has become one of the top musical events in the region.

This still doesn't explain the reaction of Bubba, who can't read the program and whose idea of good taste is a scum-fattened sewer bug.

But at the Duke Robillard concert a couple of months ago, I bought one of the famed blues musician's CDs. Bubba was asleep on the bed when I first played the disc.

Presently he came awake. By the second track he was lying on his back, swaying slightly and opening and closing his eyes as if overtaken by some sort of religious ecstasy.

By the fifth track he was actively writhing across the bed on his back, while punching his balled-up little paw-fists in the air to the sound of Duke's guitar.

This is a true story. I have witnesses.

At no time has he reacted to music as he reacted to Duke Robillard, although Kate, who baby-sits Bubba when I'm away, swears that he tries to conduct classical music recordings with his tail/baton.

I was considering taking Bubba to the Blues picnic by the lake in City Park Sunday. But as much as he likes the Dukes of the world, I fear he might prefer the ducks of the world.

And the last thing the Blues Fest organizers need is a crazed cat distracting the audience by goosing the goslings. It is his loss. He'll just have to continue listening to blues by recording rather than live.

He'll still enjoy it. And really it figures, because he does fit George Carlin's profile of being just a little — make that a lot — strange.

Critter for Hire

Bubba
Age 2
Hagerstown, Md.
e-mail: bubba@freako.com

Education: Tutored since age 6 months at the foot of one of the wisest counsels on the face of the earth. Degrees in eating, sleeping and driving people out of their skulls.

Experience: Precious little that doesn't involve being a pain in the neck. Chasing experience includes bugs, flies, squirrels, birds and stockinged feet.

Salary requirements: Weekly stipend of half-bag of catnip and some half-decayed fish. Also a $3,000 finder's fee for owner.

Well, why not? I figure since City Hall is getting into the business of hiring animals, I may as well try to make a little hay. I'm entering Bubba under the slogan "make your next bureaucrat a bureaucat."

The deal is, that because of the burgeoning waterfowl population at the lake in City Park, a committee will recommend that the City Council buy $3,000 border collie whose main job responsibility will to be to, well, go on wild goose chases.

Heck, for $3,000 — no, $2,000, a bargain — Bubba will do all the chasing you want and when you go on vacation nobody need walk him, just leave him in the closet with a little dry food and a sandbox.

Actually I'm deluding myself a bit and engaging in some false advertising. Bubba will kill, maim, chase, destroy, rip limb from limb, maul, disembowel and eviscerate any living creature you care to name — so long as there is a pane of window glass between himself and his prey.

When you remove the glass his bravery is watered down considerably and he will suddenly recall an appointment he has scheduled for this time slot underneath the bed. I don't care what military school they've attended, no cat has so thoroughly mastered the art of retreat as has Bubba.

Therefore the city may as well proceed to place Lassie under its employ — although a couple questions are floating around my tiny little brain.

First, why is it that the same people who believe it inhumane to clandestinely shake the goose eggs to decrease the surplus population believe it fine and dandy to unleash a fanged, snarling, beast to strike terror into the bosom of every feathered contrivance west of Virginia Avenue?

I understand the border collie is the type of dog that will only chase, or herd the birds and will not inflict bodily injury. But does the goose know this? "Relax mother, it's only a herding border collie. Don't let the teeth and foaming mouth fool you."

My other big question is, do border collies do crows? If so, three grand is a small price to pay.

And I do rather like the idea of having a city dog on staff. As my friend Ellen said this weekend, "At last, a public employee who works for his kibble." And he's no big strain on the pension system either.

But I suppose ole Fois Gras will have to be granted a special waiver since, technically, it's against the law to walk a dog in City Park. Which begs the question why not just let people exercise their mutts in the park and let nature take its course?

I confess to having walked Lacy in the park all the time, not aware that at any moment the dog police might swoop down and haul us off. Lacy would become very excited at the sight of the geese, although the birds regarded Lacy with the same amount of fear with which a forest fire regards a lawn sprinkler, and correctly so.

But other dogs may not be so kind. (Or inept). So to review, my solutions to reducing the goose population are, in order, lead shot; egg shaking; canine free-for-all, and finally $3,000 bird-dog specialist.

At least with the final two options the vendors can make up their lost revenue in corn sales by selling little bags of raw hamburger.

Flying in the Face of Disaster

News travels fast in a small town, and by noon I had word that a loud crash had been heard resounding from within my residence.

Most people who have been blessed with normal lives would think, "My heavens, what if a burgler has jimmied into my home and is at this minute ransacking the house and do I go home, do I call the police" and so on.

But for me, only one word wafted slowly across my mind, hanging menacingly like a threatening, black, unseeded storm cloud:

Bubba.

Bubba, the world's most passive-aggressive cat.

I ignored the entreaties of co-workers to return home, so for most of the afternoon the matter was pushed from my mind.

The matter was instantly pulled back onto my mind that evening when I opened the door.

The forensic evidence all pointed to one conclusion; no need for fiber or DNA samples here, even Dennis Fung could have figured this one out.

The contents of my house included paintings askew, vases knocked over, CDs on the floor, one carefree fly buzzing lazily around the living room and one thoroughly exhausted cat.

Of all the destructive, disastrous and idiotic things that Bubba has ever done, this ranked somewhere in the middle.

He can't catch flies and he knows he can't catch flies and he knows he looks ridiculous trying to catch flies, but does this stop him?

While I'm on the subject, two other things he does drive me nuts: He'll hoist his hind leg straight in the air like the Statue of Liberty so he can lick his stomach. Then something will distract him and he stops licking his stomach, but he forgets to put his leg down. Ten minutes later he's still lying there on the floor staring vacantly into the distance with his foot in the air. When I shower him with ridicule and abuse he just looks at me like I'm weird for not having *my* leg in the air.

The other annoying thing, and all cats do this and I believe it strikes at the heart of basic feline psychosis, is the way he looks out the window.

You know the pose, lying parallel on the sill, tail wrapped back to front, paws tucked under, head cocked 90 degrees, just staring out the window. For hours. And hours. Without moving a whisker. Waiting. Waiting for action.

I used to feel so sorry for Bubba because he would spend so many fruitless hours in the window — nothing would ever seem to happen, not even a pedestrian passing.

But then I happened to notice something. Whenever something of interest did by chance occur, Bubba, in accordance with the Prime Directive of cats never to be impressed by anything, would turn his head and refuse to watch.

It was like he spent all his time in the window waiting for something interesting to happen so he could prove to the world that he wasn't interested in it.

He's deathly scared of anyone catching him watching. A fight or something will break out and you know it's killing him not to watch, but he will turn his head away from the action and yawn as if something as mundane as a knifing couldn't possibly be on his plane of what passes for entertainment.

This pomposity from an animal that wears his fur to the bone chasing flies.

I, however, being a creature of far superior intellect, rolled up a newspaper and took after the fly myself.

Twenty minutes later the fly was still breathing, although not breathing as heavily as I was. And in flailing after the pest, I suddenly noticed that I myself had knocked a couple paintings off plumb, sent a vase flying and scattered some CDs.

I looked up at Bubba to see if he was happy now. But of course he wasn't watching.

An Early Riser

A cat has no sympathy for its ailing owner

Being under the weather is even worse for me now, because it means I have to spend the entire day with that homicidal, flea-bitten lower life form known as Bubba.

This, as they say in the State Department, is not exactly dealing from a position of strength.

He's home a lot more than I am, where he has nothing to do but think. He's also learned the terrain, so he knows all the best places to hide and wait in ambush.

Since neither of us trust each other — on the days that I have to be home we usually end up sitting on opposite sides of the room, glaring, and each waiting for the other to make the first move.

Actually, he always makes the first move, and it's always about 5:30 a.m., when he makes his first rendezvous with the cat box. This is his opening salvo, the "I'm awake and I'm going to be wanting my breakfast soon" alert. Perhaps you believe I am accusing this cat of thinking too much, of being too capable of comprehending the rules of logic, reasoning, premeditation and stratagem.

To which I would reply that no cat needs to make so much noise when using a cat box. It sounds like he's dumping a load of marbles into a 55-gallon steel drum. And time? He fiddles around in that box long enough to plant an entire Victory Garden. Don't tell me he doesn't know what he's about.

By 6, if I still haven't gotten up, he starts in on the metal mini blinds, raking his claws up and down like some Aboriginal call to battle. Then it's off to the cardboard scratching box. I'd never thought of cardboard as a particularly noisy commodity until I got Bubba. But give him three minutes and lights will start popping on throughout the neighborhood.

Notice up til now there hasn't been a bit of physical or verbal assault. That's Phase II, when he stomps all over my back and begins to meow in my ear. Actually, it's less a meow than it is a quack. And it's not pleasant, but I can on occasion ignore even this — especially if I've just gone to bed about four hours earlier.

But then he applies the *coup de grace*, something he knows I cannot stand in the least. He alights on the dining room table and summarily begins batting solid objects off onto the hardwood floor — pens, CD cases, silverware.

It drives me absolutely bats. Especially, and this proves the dark, insidious and evil essence of his soul, since he never knocks them off in any type of one-after-the-other rhythm that you could used to and sleep through.

No, it's "CLANK." Then you wait, and wait and wait. And just when you think there must be nothing more in the table and you're drifting back to sle... "CLATTER."

And this is all before the sun has even come up.

You can imagine what the rest of the day is like. He doesn't particularly like to be touched. He refuses to do any chores. His solution to everything is to bite.

Last week he got hold of a brand-new, unopened 20-pound bag of cat food and shredded it, consuming who knows how many of the 20 pounds. Then when I got home he had the audacity to cry for more food.

I pointed out there was food all around him. He was positively swimming in food. But did this argument change his mind? Oh no. I think he wanted canned.

So anyway, by the end of the day, I was pretty well frazzled. Then I remembered the three words I knew would extract a sweet dose of revenge:

Westminster Kennel Club.

I made Bubba watch the annual dog show on TV, and I must say, he demonstrated considerable interest. Unfortunately, this was day one, when they show off the tiny breeds. Bubba now believes that a dog is an odd-looking, funnily shorn animal about half his size.

If there were one thing this cat didn't need, it was another shot of self-confidence.

One In, One Out

I hate going to the mall on a Friday night. That's because I love teenagers, and your chances of seeing any at that time and place are practically nil. But go I did last weekend, and I came away with an even higher regard for teens than I had before.

I was accompanying my friend, who had some shopping to do for a wedding shower. This was embarrassing enough — me, standing in the nightie section of Penney's, saying things like "You're kidding, they put lace there?" (My friend theorized that the reason half of our marriages end in divorce is because of weird delicates).

And in the fragrance store, where my friend uneasily asked for a "passion-scented candle." The clerk gave her a long, measured, baleful look which said a lot of things, but can basically be summed up with

"Why, you slut." Which left us hastily and unconvincingly saying as how it wasn't for us, it was for a friend's wedding shower, etc., etc.

Anyway, since my friend has a key to the apartment building, and since I seldom lock my own door (I probably shouldn't have announced that) I left my own keys home. Which would not ordinarily have been a problem, had it not been for a certain storm sewer grate and I bet you can guess where I'm going with this.

Yes, she was giving me her keys to drive, but it was not what is known in football circles as a "clean hand-off." In what took two seconds but seemed like two hours, the keys fell to the ground, started sliding, stopped and asked directions, then gleefully headed straight for, and down into, the grate.

The good news was that it wasn't a particularly deep grate. We could see them glinting and laughing at us from down below in the streetlight. With proper tools they could probably be fished out.

The bad news was that the proper tools, along with my own keys, were inside the apartment building, which was locked drum-tight.

This necessitated an assault on the side of the apartment building to a second-story window. I made it to a fire-escape landing, popped the lock and assumed the worst to be over.

But I hadn't counted on Bubba.

The cat was front and center, alert and interested, and of a mood to cause difficulties. Every time I'd make a lunge to get in, he'd make a lunge to get out. I hope nobody has this on videotape.

I'd jump, he'd jump, I'd let go of the sill, catch him, throw him back then catch myself back on the landing. We went through this exercise about four times, with Bubba showing no signs of tiring from the repetition.

And of course this was one of those guillotine windows that won't stay open without a prop. So there I am, the window going after my throat, me hanging off the landing, the cat hanging off me and I was starting to get really annoyed. Finally I propped open the window with Bubba then shielded him with a screen and then screen, cat and myself all rolled into the kitchen in a tangle of fur, wire and blood.

I emerged on the street a minute later armed with a coat hanger, flashlight and kitchen tongs, where I found my friend surrounded by three teenage boys.

I was considering the distinct military disadvantage of having to defend ourselves with tongs when the fellows grabbed all three appurtenances and went diving after the keys as if they were their own. On my word, I have never met three more eagerly helpful young men in my life. They retrieved the keys in an instant, and I wish I knew their names.

If you are reading this guys, thank you. And as for everyone else, I think the moral of this story is crystal clear: Never go to the mall shopping for passion candles without your keys unless you first tie up your cat.

Whose Cat is Worst?

Would anyone want to trade a ferret for a cat?

Who'd have thought? Rasha the Ferret made it all the way to the Supreme Court.

Rasha, you remember, met an unfortunate demise at the hands of the health department after the pet bit a kid and had to be tested for rabies.

The only way to test a critter for the disease is to pull a Henry VIII, and heads not being reattatchable appendages as a general thing, it meant the end of the ferret.

Of course you can understand the thinking of the family of the girl who was bitten. This an animal's health versus a person's health, and in such cases you always have to side with the person, unless the person happens to be a paid health-insurance industry lobbyist.

But the owners of the ferret believed the pet was seized with no review of whether it was even possible for Rasha to have the disease (it didn't). Therefore, they sought compensation for the seizure of private property. But the high court refused to hear the case.

But just that the Supreme Court had the opportunity to hear a ferret case. How cool would it have been to hear arguments for Rasha the Ferret vs. The United States?

My contract states that here I must interject the thought that this would be no big deal since the Supreme Court justices listen to ferrets arguing before them all the time. But the obviousness of the joke, coupled with the fact that I still feel remorseful for already picking on lawyers once this week, doesn't make me feel good about it.

Continuing on the animal theme (a colleague recently said she likes it better when I write about animals than when I write about politicians. To my credit, I held my tongue), I was wondering whether anyone might wish to trade a ferret for a cat.

This after Bubba, the world's most dangerous cat, spent all of Monday night systematically and deliberately shredding piles of newspapers. I didn't care about the papers so much, but the noise made it impossible to sleep. I threw at him shoes, books, a bottle of hand cream, a hair brush and a couple of candlesticks, but he just took this for applause and congratulations. In the morning I was totally zonked and he was proudly sitting in the middle of a mountain of tattered paper, like he'd been up all night playing tip jars.

But do I receive any sympathy? Hmph. To date, my mail has been 100 percent pro-Bubba. Two examples:

Jackie Renee Coblentz of Jefferson, Md., said that next to her cat Sambu, Bubba is, well, a pussycat. Sambu's trick is to wait until she's asleep, then scratch on the door to get out. Having that inner sense, as all cats are born with, of when a person has just gotten back to sleep, he'll then scratch to come back in. And of course this is just a warming up — a sort of light calisthenics before the real terrorism begins.

And Judy Russell of Ijamsville, Md., tended to agree. "Bubba is a real lightweight when it comes to being an alarm clock," she wrote. "Big Max, who weighs 19 pounds could give classes on awaking humans. Although Bubba demonstrates some fairly sophisticated techniques, you should give Bubba a treat for being reasonable about the whole thing."

After reading the rest of the letter, included vivid descriptions that I won't frighten your children with here, I agree she might be right.

But remember, Bubba is 14 months old. He's kind of like the Tiger Woods of the tour. No one can say how bad he has the potential to be. So to Jackie, Judy and the rest, let's give it a year and compare notes. Knowing Bubba, I predict a breakthrough year in terms of feline atrocities — and I'd be willing to make this case before the Supreme Court.

Bubba, Forever Young

I could leave the door open in between trips to the car. I could put bags on the floor without fear of a Cruise Missile diving into the plastic and emerging at double speed with a powder white face full of flour. Nor did I have to chase plastic bags through the house as they noisily crackled from room to room, propelled by a terrified animal devoid of the first clue about how to extract himself.

No one ate the lettuce, no one crushed the pasta, no one batted the sponges under the fridge.

It was all pretty glum.

Bubba had a way of turning something as routine as unloading groceries into an event that would make the 1965 Watts riots look like a senior citizen craft fair.

Some sick part of me enjoyed this, and I was actually saddened to think of the day when he would become old and tired and act like a plain-old-cat cat, lying for hours in the sun or in a lap with only the infrequent catnip-induced spasm.

But then one day he did start acting like a plain old cat. He moped around, sleeping most of the day and refusing to eat. He was a shadow of himself, a black and white photograph of a black and white cat once so demonic that those two seemed the most vibrant, explosive colors on earth. I even bought a black and white checked bedspread so he'd match (an exercise indicative less of my decorating skills than of my disdain for the daily vacuuming of bedspreads).

Bubba, a talker and a dancer, did his best to keep up. He'd yap at me in a weak voice and slowly lift first his left paw and then his right in his unique feline two-step. But there was no recovery. Bubba died a week later of a liver tumor — died stoically, rather reflectively I

44

thought, as if contemplating whether it had been wise to use up 15 years worth of energy in slightly less than three.

The cat never was one to think about things until after he did them. Two thirds of the way to the ground from the top of the refrigerator his eyes might betray a flicker of recognition that a safer course might have availed itself had he looked, although by then of course it was too late to void the contract.

But even if the results were less than positive, he never showed regret, so I suppose he was content that he whooped it up while he could and left this world like JFK — forever young.

Cats do to one's intellect what a strong-fingered pastry chef does to dough, kneading and mushing it beyond all recognizable structure, form and logic. What else would inspire a relatively balanced individual to compare an animal with a president of the United States? (Stop that, I know what you're thinking.)

Yet Bubba, as all cats, I imagine, transcended convention in a furry sort of way. He would see a meticulously frosted chocolate devil's-food cake balanced delicately in a windowsill above a basket full of freshly laundered pastel towels and say "Why not?"

While he was around I was comforted knowing that at worst I was only the second-weirdest life form on the planet. And he comforted me by showing that eccentricity and dignity are not mutually exclusive. Bless him, he had fun.

The evening before he got sick Bubba, for no discernible reason, streaked up behind me, launched himself off the patio and did a midair 180-degree spin. He landed facing me, his eyes a mix of confusion, embarrassment and defiance. He didn't know why he'd done it, but he did it, so there. He stretched, flicked his ears back and trotted off.

A week later he was drifting off for the last time on the stainless steel table. I gave him one last scratch on the ears before my wonderful vet (the cat's, I mean) covered him gently with a towel.

Half a minute after he should have been gone, Bubba gave one last, tremendous lurch. The final exclamation point of a dying clown. Poor boy.

Even Jake Biscuit Deserted Me on Cat Question

I'm sorry about this. I am really, truly sorry. No one hates "What my pet did last night" columns more than me. I understand that they are sophomoric, tedious and virtually unreadable. So if you wish to move on to some story about how planes on the Hagerstown-Pittsburgh connection are being downsized to crop dusters that do loop-de-loops enroute, I will understand.

But writing is my psychiatrist's couch and when something pains me, it is the only vehicle I have for cleansing my soul, if any.

It all began (dream sequence) about two weeks ago when the four-footed annoyance named Jake Biscuit began to develop a lively interest in something that was underneath the house. I hesitate to comment on Jake's mental configuration because I do not wish to get sued by a dog, but suffice to say that Jake has a lot of "imaginary friends."

Or imaginary enemies, I should say. He's always wanting to kill things that don't exist, so I didn't pay his actions much mind. But his opinion was unfortunately validated about a week later when a little tike who had just gotten off the school bus came up to me and said, Ralph Wiggum style, "Mister, your back porch is mewing."

And sure enough it was, although mewing is too kind a term. Bellowing is more like it. RowRowRow, sort of like an ambulance.

At first I ignored it, sort of the way you ignore an unfamiliar sound coming from your car engine, hoping it will go away. It didn't. It was a cat and it wasn't going anywhere.

All cats that have tried to adopt us in the past have been stupid. They have either nuzzled up to young Alexa (bad) or myself (worse), acts that for differing reasons have turned out to be poor career decisions.

But this cat knew instinctively that it is the Doctor Doolittle in High Heels who calls the shots around our house, and when she called him, he immediately came out from underneath the porch and jumped into her arms. Ten seconds later, I — with head down and shoulders sagging — was sent out for cat food.

The animal has the most amazing mane of long, flowing white hair, so I said "Look, if we're going to keep him, I am going to insist that we name him Peter Gammons."

Of course the dog probably had a better chance of knowing who the great baseball analyst Peter Gammons is (if you've never seen him, think Andrew Jackson) than the two females in the house, so we compromised. With all that white fur, and because we were dining on fried chicken that night, we finally settled on calling him Colonel Sanders. Kind of cosmic, everyone said.

A stray kitten that has been both fed and named is all but a family member, but I still had an ace up my sleeve, the aforementioned Jake Biscuit. I saw no way he would be content to play second fiddle to some glorified dust mop, and he held the deciding vote. If they didn't get along, the cat would have to go.

The next day, the family took the Colonel to the vet. It depressed me further when they came back enthusiastic.

"He's four months old, and get this, the vet thinks he's mostly Himalayan."

"Mostly which?"

"Himalayan. It's a breed of cat."

"Oh come on, who's going to dump a Himalayan? It's not like I've been seeing a lot of Sherpas hanging out at Sheetz."

"And everyone just loved him. A couple people wanted to buy him."

"WHAT? They wanted to... And you didn't... And we still have... How much did they offer?"

"Oh I don't know, they just said 'how much do you want for him,' and..."

At this point, I had fainted dead away on the kitchen floor, so the rest of her comment is lost to the ages. Worse, the stupid dog was of absolutely no assistance whatsoever. The one time I wanted him to be a jerk, and it turns out he loves the cat, too.

I swear, he wanted to show off. He made us throw his ball, and then he'd practically jump up out of his skin in front the cat all hyper and ecstatic like. "Look at me! I can fetch the ball! Did you see me? Did you see? I can fetch the ball!"

Entirely unimpressed, the Colonel just sat there stone-faced and then cast a slow, baleful glance up at us, silently asking if this embarrassing creature made a habit of sacrificing his dignity through such shameful displays. Which, of course, he does.

I haven't had a cat since the late Bubba, but it looks as if I have one now. When I wake up or get home, the cat is yowling to be fed and the dog is whining to go out and if I pet one the other gets jealous and life just keeps getting more complicated. So if you have a pet bird you're tired of, please don't dump it in my neighborhood.

Time to Tangle with Birds Again

If the avian flu ever hits Hagerstown, we may as well activate the ole "do not resuscitate" orders posthaste, because birds have taken over our property.

We like birds OK, I guess, although we did not go out or our way to create a bird sanctuary. It just turns out that Da Birds and us happen to like the same things — trees, statuary, berry-producing shrubs, bug-rich gardens, water features. We got bird baths because they were ornamental; who knew birds actually used the things? If you get a sundial with Roman numerals, you don't expect to see dudes in togas sitting around it.

While I have no particular anti-bird agenda, I do like them to know that rules are rules. There are people things and there are bird things and I oppose any of the so-called twain-meetings.

So when I returned recently from the Great White (literally, unfortunately) North to discover the strawberries ripening and the birds licking their chops I hauled out the estimated 17 square acres of bird netting I keep in the shed for just such occasions.

It deters most of the species, but we have a couple of particularly lawless robins who clearly have problems with authority.

We were sitting on the back porch over the weekend, when a friend noted matter-of-factly that "a bird just got under your net."

Not a man to allow contempt of court on the part of a robin, I used my gazelle-like speed to lumber off in the direction of the strawberry patch.

I need to stop here and mention that what should have been one pretty much standard bird eviction was complicated by the presence of the dog named Jake Biscuit, who also was outside at the time.

There has never been a fight that he hasn't wanted to be fully involved in, and without thinking I poured fuel on the fire by yelling, "Get him, boy."

In matters of war, Jake is a dog that doesn't have to be told twice. Sensing the excitement of the moment, he threw back his ears and pawed the ground with a fierceness, advancing on the quarry at a speed that was, regretfully, much greater than my own.

By this time the bird had discovered that he was the subject of a writ of *habeas chirpus*, and was making every effort to rediscover the slit in the net through which the B&E had been facilitated. He didn't find it. Instead he became hopelessly tangled and panicked, flapping and cheeping furiously, and cursing the man who invented mesh.

Maybe you have been in a situation where events are unfolding faster than you would like them to, and you only have time to express your worst fears in half a fleeting thought before the world comes crashing down.

This is what happened here, and as I watched Jake streaking toward the netted strawberry cage, I clearly remember thinking to myself:

"Say, that dog wouldn't be stupid enough to ..."

Well, of course, investing in intelligence futures with Jake won't make many millionaires. The animal did indeed launch himself with full force at the flapping and fussing bird-tornado, which obviously he did not get because obviously a dog is just as subject to the rules of bird-net physics as is a robin.

In an instant, the population of frantically entangled life forms on my property had doubled.

And it was about to triple, since my presence was required in the nylon fray to try to sort things all out. And right in the middle of all the nets and dogs and birds and fits and screeches and howls and yips and fur and feathers and claws and beaks whirling about me in blender-like ferocity, it did — I admit it — flash across my mind that just two scant days ago I had been sitting atop a mountain in a shining sun and cool breeze with a view of lakes and mountains that went on forever with nary a sound or trouble on the radar.

Welcome home, I guess.

The event played itself out. All parties, I believe, would admit that mistakes were made. But no one was killed or wounded. I trudged back to the porch, awaiting what I knew would be some sarcastic witticism from the grandstand.

But no one said not a word concerning the event. I was kind of itching to know, but didn't want to ask. Did anyone see my humiliation as funny? Ridiculous? Pathetic? I didn't know. I still don't.

Their expressions blank as a refrigerator door, they simply remained quiet and continued to gaze calmly over the yard, as if nothing odd or unusual had occurred at all.

Sadly, perhaps it hadn't.

Split, Not Jake, Superb at Catching Thingee That Soars

I tried, heaven knows I tried. I made him sleep with a Frisbee, I fed him in a Frisbee, I made the Frisbee his constant companion.

But Jake Biscuit never mastered the Frisb — I mean, he never mastered the plastic flying disc. Sorry, for a second there I forgot that I worked for a newspaper (Industry Motto: "Trying to Confuse You With Vague Product Descriptions — Such as 'Canned Aerosol Cheese-Like Substance' So We Don't Have To Mention Brand Names,' Since 1833").

So when you saw the headlines last week that a Hagerstown dog had won the flying-disc-catching contest at the Great Outdoor Games,

I hope you didn't for a second think it might have been Jake.

The winner was in fact a dog named Split, a border collie owned by Hagerstown's Ron Watson. He said there is an amazing connection — Ron said this, not Split — between dog and man that allows for such a finely choreographed pitch and airborne catch.

"It's like you're quarterbacking, and you have Randy Moss doing tricks and backflips," Watson told *The Herald-Mail's* Karen Hanna following the competition.

I've seen the footage, and just like Randy Moss, Split also wagged his bare tush at the crowd. Actually, I haven't seen the footage because I'm writing on Friday and the show didn't air on ESPN until Saturday. I don't want to create a Mitch Albom situation here. But I just assume he wagged, because all dogs do.

Even Jake. But catch, he could not. The dog is fast as lightning, so tracking was no problem. But he would always wait for it to settle gently — barking at it insanely, as a general thing — to the ground before snapping it up and furiously pounding back to me like some kind of miniature Pony Express.

I would sit there for hours, minutes actually, puzzling over how to get it through the animal's lemon that I wanted him to grab the flying disc before it hit the ground. But there is no good way to explain things to a dog.

I would even put the Frisbee in my own teeth, after wiping it off, of course, with a boxed facial paper tissue product. I tried tossing it to him at short distance, but it would just hit him between the eyes — an event that, for some reason, seemed to make him enormously happy.

Plying the waters of Jake's cognitive processes always put me at risk of capsizing, so I fell back on sheer repetition. 'Course that didn't work, for reasons that anyone who has ever owned a terrier will understand.

After a half-dozen tosses, Jake stopped contemplating the Frisbee as a component of recreation, and began to contemplate it as an component of diet. He would flop under the nearest tree and commence chewing, and by the time he got around to returning it, the disc's aerodynamics had been severely compromised.

Watson said he made the switch to the brainy border collies because "... I wanted a smart dog. My dog as a child was an idiot, a complete idiot."

Ron. I know the feeling.

In fact, my only shot at ESPN is if they come up with a contest to see which dog can stare uninterrupted for the most number of hours into a chipmunk hole.

Anyway, this made us look good on ESPN and it was also good news for people who like to watch bizarre sports over the weekend.

Although not quite as bizarre, I dare say, as one that was scheduled at Martinsburg's Motorcycle Mania Bike Week: Coleslaw wrestling. (Can I say Coleslaw, or would that be "shredded cabbage, carrot and homogenized egg solids product?")

Jeff Wilkins, organizer of the bike week, says he's been flooded with requests from people looking to get in on the pit that will contain 500 pounds of coleslaw and 150 pounds of vegetable oil. Me? I don't know. Seeing women wrestle in coleslaw is all right, I guess, although personally I've always preferred creamed corn. Just a question of artistic preference, I suppose.

Either way it should be fun. The only down side that I can see is that newspaper photo-caption writers throughout the Tri-State will be salivating to write: "I fought the slaw and the slaw won."

Indeed. One couple even wants to get married in the side dish. That's rich. What do you exchange, vows or salad forks? Who performs the ceremony, a preacher or a cafeteria worker?

"Dearly beloved, we are gathered here together in the presence of mayonnaise..." Just remember, guys, 40 years from now you have to show the photos to the grandkids. Do you really want them to see you there on your wedding day thigh deep in cabbage, wearing a Hooters T-shirt and hoisting a Budweiser — I'm sorry, a carbonated malted beverage product?

A Cheerful, Optimistic Nuisance

A dog, people say, is a constant companion.

And they say it like that's a good thing.

Which it normally is, I grant you, unless you are highly diseased and laid up in bed and turning your neck 30 degrees to the left takes the energy normally associated with carrying three bags of cement to Poland.

Jake Biscuit was extra excited, because he assumed I had stayed home last week expressly to be with him. And when I say "extra excited," you will realize that this is not easy since he is a Jack Russell Terrier and to think of a Jack Russell as "extra" anything is a frightening prospect indeed. Like saying that last week Enron was "extra deceitful."

Occasionally Jake will slow down to the speed of nuclear fission, but that doesn't happen often. He can outrun a squirrel, outdig a mole, outjump a cat and outwhine Mary Matalin.

Jake is very cute, as people always point out after he has committed some atrocity that transgresses the bounds of what a reasonable man should have to endure. And he is. And of course we love each other dearly. Usually.

Each day he greets me when I get home from work my shoving a ball into the sensitive area just below the kneecap. (He's not very big — white with a brown head and tail with a white stripe running down the length of his nose), And he won't rest until I have taken him outside and thrown the ball for him an estimated 50 million times. But does this tire him out? Oh no. This is for a warmup. He has many other items on his agenda for which he demands an accomplice - and if I fail as a co-conspirator and dare to want to go in the house and lie down, he has a standing army of vocal persuasion tactics including, but not limited to, yelp, cry, whine, yip and out-and-out shriek.

So anyway, all of this I can pretty much deal with on a normal day —but as mentioned, last week was not normal. At every turn of consciousness, there he would be, ball in mouth, hopefully shoving it up at the bed (I could never let my hand carelessly fall over the edge of the bed for it would be immediately and enthusiastically slimed).

As I said, he is so cute and with those big brown eyes of his looking up at me like the hungry eyes of a small, dirty-faced child in some Dickens tale, it is very hard to say no.

It is also very useless to say no. While cute and friendly, he is not the brightest dog in the world and to him, "no" is a word that he must equate with "by all means, Jake, I will comply to your every demand post haste."

Jake in fact knows two words, exactly: "Ball" and "Bath." Utter the former, he will jump out of his skin. Utter the latter and he will disappear for about two minutes until his little 3-hp brain forgets that you said it. He has a vague, theoretical idea of the word "come." And, bless his heart, he does try. Say "Jake, come" and he will stop what he's doing, tilt his head quizzically and search the memory banks of the old bean like he just knows that the word has some relevance, but for the life of him he can't bring to bear what it is.

So last week, my defenses were left to this. Every so often I would rasp the word "bath" and then try to drift off for a couple minutes until he came back more eager than before.

But he was cheerful, and last week I needed all the cheerful I could gut. Jake Biscuit. I think we'll keep him.

Jack Russell on Ice, Shaken, Not Stirred

A couple of weeks ago, we had about three inches of snow. Then, the ground-surface plummeted to 20 degrees, while up in the stratosphere, the air warmed into the mid-30s. Along comes a major storm system, in which precipitation from way up high fell as rain, but froze upon hitting the earth's surface, creating a quarter-inch crust of solid ice on top of the existing snow.

As any weatherman can tell you, these are the perfect meteorological conditions to own a dog.

Not a reserved or careful dog, but one of those energetic, edgy, hyperactive, Joan Rivers dogs. An act-first, think-second dog. Not a wise and philosophical dog, but an unschooled and utterly pigheaded dog who believes he can alter the rules of nature and physics through the sheer force of his will.

Enter Jake Biscuit.

As has been well-documented here, this is a Jack Russell terrier who defines the term "wound a little too tight" in its purest sense. He is less Jack Russell than he is Jack Hammer. Say the word "outside" (the only two-syllable word in the English language that he's been able to noodle through) and he sets about whining and quivering and his eyes bug out like a cartoon coyote. In fact, he is the only dog I know of that can break out in an anticipatory sweat.

The cat named Colonel Sanders — who could teach Henry Kissinger a thing or two about dignity — will watch this performance with the disdain of a parent whose youngster recently has discovered rap.

After watching the dog for a few seconds with a sour expression, the cat slowly will turn his head to look at one of us, as if we are responsible for this atrocity and really should consider putting him out of this peculiar ecstatic misery once and for all.

The instant the door actually opens, the dog catapults into the world at large with the force of a thousand cannons, although about 10 feet into the journey, he will slam full on the brakes because he, at that point, has realized he has forgotten his ball. At this point, the animal nearly splits in two, so great is the anguish at the dilemma he faces.

Should he run back inside to get his ball, there's a chance the door could close behind him and his shot at the great outdoors will be lost. On the other hand — what good is the outdoors without a ball? So he stands there, straining mightily in both directions and fretting terribly over a problem that clearly is bigger than he is.

But — and call me a kindhearted pet owner if you must — on days when there is a thick crust of ice on the snow, I always MAKE SURE he has his ball beforehand.

This is not sport on my part. I mean, he has to be exercised, right? And his preferred method of physical exertion is to fetch a ball, no? Therefore, who am I to deprive him of his most deeply cherished activity? And if others feel differently, well excuse me for being the nice guy that I am.

So I launch the tennis ball.

It arcs over the frozen snow, and Jake Biscuit will take a deep breath of oxygen and then fly out of the shoveled path on his way to the prize. It all works out as he's planned it for the first second and a half. The complications set in with his first course correction. Being a trained varmint pursuer, he's bred to turn on a dime. And he expects to turn on a dime. But with ice underneath, it is worth the price of admission to watch as this dime turns into a quarter, then a dollar, then a $20 and in a split second into all of Fort Knox.

His tiny little brain has calculated 20 degrees left, and for the life of him he can't understand why he still is going straight. The animal is not designed to cognitively negotiate environmental factors; all he knows is to try to turn harder. So he sets the turn at 30 degrees. Still, no response. Angry now, he tries for a more severe angle.

It's usually when he passes 45 degrees that disaster strikes.

At this point, any semblance of control vanishes and he begins to spin like Dorothy Hamill. I confess to feeling a touch of guilt here because with each 360, his eyes for the briefest of instants will catch mine in a forlorn plea for me to *do* something.

But it is too late. Too many variations are in play. Each paw gets conflicting messages from the brain and they end up going in four different directions until they give out completely and he belly-flops onto the ice and off he slides into the distance, past my neighbor's house, past my neighbor's neighbor's house, past my neighbor's neighbor's neighbor's house, until he disappears altogether behind a far-off hedge.

Some time later, he'll come gingerly tiptoeing back. He will have retrieved the ball — he's too proud not to — but he has lost his taste for the game. Pity, because I haven't.

With a View to a Kill — Jake Biscuit Style

It's said that killers will always kill again, but in the case of the feisty Jack Russell terrier named Jake Biscuit, three years had passed since his winning encounter with a squirrel, so I had hoped his taste for blood had passed.

Jake is 6 this summer, and has lost a step and gained a pound. Or 12. His Wild Animal Elimination Project has also flagged, falling victim to the realization — earned at the price of four long years of research — that rabbits and squirrels are faster than he is.

A couple of times, he did try to sink his teeth into his foes not through superior speed, but through superior intellect. But he made a failure of it.

It was, however, interesting to watch. Jake decided that maybe the rabbit would not run away if he (the rabbit) thought that he (the dog) did not see him (the rabbit). A cunning stratagem, and one that he must have been working on for years in his tiny little dog brain, much as Andy Dufresne plotted his escape from Shawshank.

One day, Jake spotted a rabbit on the far end of the property, as evidenced by his ears taking a rapid hitch to the north. But this time he didn't engage his normal "streak across the yard at full speed barking at the top of his lungs" response. No, this was the smarter, craftier Jake.

Being careful not to make any direct eye contact with the bunny, he slowly stood up, yawned and ambled off the porch with a, "Gee it's a nice day, I think I'll take a little stroll" air about him. He struck out in a noncommittal direction that brought him closer to the rabbit by diagonal degrees, but was by no means a direct path. He walked over to a flowerbed and sniffed at a rose bush; then over to the herb garden where he sat down to scratch.

So earnest and heartfelt was his dedication to this strategy that it almost brought tears to my eyes. He could have been criticized for overacting, I suppose, but truly, it was by a country mile the most layered thought process I had ever seen this dog engage.

He was gaining on his quarry slowly, at the rate of maybe 10 feet a minute, but it was with overdone casualness, like a preacher whistling in a porn shop. Beneath his skin, you could see his muscles ticing and quivering as he called on every ounce of self-restraint to keep himself in check. He never once turned his head directly toward his target, but his eyeballs were straining at their corners with such force I feared that if his ocular tendons were to shear, his eyes would come popping out of his head like Champaign corks.

The rabbit, meanwhile, was watching this performance with considerable interest, which of course was not the intention. Sad to say, but if anything, Jake was attracting even more attention to himself with his little trampoline act, and when the dog deemed himself close enough to lunge, the rabbit was way ahead of him.

Jake was in an unspeakably sour mood for days after this happened. Brain having failed him, he reverted to brawn, chasing every living thing for all he was worth.

My neighbor Charlie was watching him last week when Jake finally scored, but there were, as they say, "circumstances," and you will have to judge for yourself whether this should be judged as a legitimate kill.

According to Charlie, as the mist lifted on the morning of 23 June, Jake Biscuit found himself confronted not by one rabbit, but two. Hopelessly outnumbered, the brave dog nevertheless charged the closest one, which obligingly zigged and zagged and doubled back, keeping comfortably ahead of the frothing canine at 6 o'clock.

Rabbit B, meanwhile, seemed perfectly content to sit and watch the drama play out, figuring either that this wasn't his battle or that his brethren was in no serious danger.

He was right on the second count.

The battleground shifted, however, when Rabbit A's evacuation route took him a little too close to Rabbit B's defensive position. For whatever reason, Rabbit B did not see this as a potential problem. And honestly it shouldn't have been, because when Jake gets an idea in his head, he's never demonstrated any inclination toward mental flexibility.

But just this poor rabbit's luck, Thursday turned out to be the one day that Jake was able to think outside the box.

Charlie said that Jake, under a full head of steam, was almost past the sitting rabbit when at the last second, he reached over and snatched it off its haunches, slicker than a frog snapping up a mosquito.

There's been no living with this dog since. His opinion of himself has never been small, and now it's off the charts. And he's probably fueled for another three years of critter chasing, although if you were to poll the neighborhood small animal association, I doubt that a substantial percentage is concerned.

Dog Fails Rabbit Test

Even as a tiny child who was supposed to cotton to small furry animals, I remember taking the side of Farmer McGregor over his archenemy, Peter Rabbit.

I don't know why especially, except that even at that tender age my keen sense of justice already had me recognizing hard work and industry over mooching freeloaders. Or perhaps I was simply having a 40-year-premature premonition.

Come to think of it, Bugs Bunny may be the only rabbit in pop culture that I have openly supported. The Easter Bunny always seemed something of a cold fish to me, the Energizer Bunny is too smug, the Volkswagen Rabbit too small, Harvey the Rabbit too big and Br'er Rabbit too disingenuous.

But Peter was the worst, sort of the welfare mom of rabbits, getting fat on the public trough, a gluttonous thief that even the ACLU would have a hard time defending.

For the record, I was sort of ambivalent about Flopsy and Mopsy, although they were a bit too conformist for my taste. There has to be a good middle ground for rabbits, in my opinion, between the milquetoast, kowtow-to-authority Flopsy and the pathologically villainous Peter.

But I digress.

The point is, jumping to present times, that this is the first year my vegetable garden has fired on all cylinders. Before, it was always too wet, too dry, too buggy, too weedy, or the soil was of the wrong acidity, or I had planted too soon or too late, or in the wrong phase of Aquarius, or something.

With gardens, when you must "rest your case" on a couple of spindly tomato plants and that barroom brawler of vegetables, the zucchini, the animals don't pay you much mind.

I put a fence around my garden, but it was mostly delusional — something to make me falsely believe there was something within its confines that a wild, starving animal might actually want.

This year there is use for a fence, but of course mine is no good because I used too large a "mesh," meaning my fence will keep out caribou and some of the larger species of walrus, but nothing smaller.

Enter the baby bunny. Literally.

Everyone knows what a rabbit can do to a row of green beans, so I'll spare you the damage report and go straight to my eradication policy, which I believe would be pretty effective, were not half of it dependent upon a highly incompetent Jack Russell terrier by the name of Jake Biscuit.

Let me say right off that he is in my employ for marketing purposes only. I believe I could easily have slaughtered the bunny myself, except that in my female-intensive household, when a wild-eyed madman with a hoe is pitted against a cute, furry little animal, the public-opinion polls skew heavily in favor of the critter.

This is not right, but facts are facts, so I mended the battle plan with the cunning stratagem of pitting beast against beast. If I kill a rabbit, I will be forever scorned, but if Jake exercises the contract the thinking will be more along the lines of "well, that's what dogs do." I figured he'd get off light, with maybe a finger shake and a "bad dog" rap, and I'd skate home free.

The dog, of course, knew when the rabbit was in the garden and he would hop up against the fence and yip and shriek and carry on like Roger Moore at a Haliburton board meeting, so when the alarm was thus sounded I'd grab the hoe and begin to probe the thick rows of foliage.

Eventually I'd flush out the beast, and he'd wriggle through the fence, where Jake was supposed to send him to that great carrot patch in the sky. 'Course that didn't work.

Neighbors would watch rather uneasily as I would yell "There he is, there he is! Get him! He's right there! No, don't look at my hand, look over there! He's getting away — you, you idiot!"

One of the tragedies of America, and I think someone needs to address this, is that even in a land with riches and abundance such as ours, there are not enough synonyms for the word "stupid" in our common language to fully describe the mental capacities of Jake Biscuit.

We played out the same thing over and over about a million times and never once did he noodle it through that the rabbit would be exiting the garden right on the heels of my hoe. For some strange reason, he always thought he ought to cover the side opposite from me.

Once the bunny did make the tactical mistake of changing course and exiting right in front of the dog and Jake bellowed out a war cry and came down with the Mother of All Chomps ... and missed.

As Charlie Brown would say, *Sigh*. Store-bought green beans, here I come.

Jake Biscuit Finally Gets the Best of the Cat

It's hard being a cat. You have to walk this fine line between disinterested dignity on one hand and, on the other, letting everyone know exactly what's on your mind.

Take the case of Colonel Sanders who, in the space of 30 seconds this week, went from being sound asleep on a file cabinet to being locked in a cage on his way to the vet.

Apparently this was a date the colonel had neglected to mark on his calendar, because he was caught entirely off-guard, which was kind of the point.

With the clean, ruthless efficiency of a hostage-taking, I had him in the truck before he was able to clear the cobwebs.

For an animal that regards himself in the same exclusive company as the Sacred Cat of Sekhmet, this was too much. What appeared to put him over the top was the fact that the dog named Jake Biscuit was taking such obscene, tail-wagging pleasure in seeing the cat laid low.

Jake, the dog with the brain made up of gossamer and Tinkertoys, is always two or three steps behind the cat, and is always falling into the colonel's traps — like falling asleep under a chair, unaware that there's a cat atop, lying in wait of the first snore to give him a good round bat in the chops, just on general principles.

But this is not a hard dog to fool. It's taken him five years to conclude that rabbits, as a breed, are faster than he is and to develop an alternative strategy. Two weeks ago, some ancient instinct in the dog took over, and when he spied a rabbit, Jake stretched himself out and raised his left paw in a classic "point."

So low are my expectations at this stage, that I heaped praise on him for successfully completing a basic maneuver that most normal dogs have successfully performed since they were pups.

If he'd stopped there, he'd have been fine. But he took the applause as reason to increase the performance, and raised a second paw in the air. This might — I doubt it, but it might — have worked, had he raised his fore port paw and the aft starboard paw. As it was, however, both ports, front and rear, went airborne.

It's funny how in the space of about three-quarters of a second, you can see a million things happening.

The first was the flash of illumination across the animal's face that "something's wrong." And then, "but what?"

Given the material she had to work with, it was about all we could have expected of the trainer to hammer "sit," "come" and "fetch" into his tiny little brain. There was simply no time left in the course to explain to him the fundamental laws of gravity and elemental physics.

The proposition that he would probably be OK if he would only return one of his two skyward paws to earth apparently never formed a blip on his mental radar screen.

As he felt his equilibrium slipping away, he did what he always does when he's in a tight place. He cast one fleeting, over-the-shoulder glance back at me in a silent, pathetic plea for assistance. Of course, there was nothing I could do but watch as he ingloriously toppled over on his side, like a bicyclist who has forgotten to loosen his toe straps.

So obviously, this is not an animal that the cat likes to see gain the upper hand. Colonel Sanders, of course, couldn't say anything in front of the dog for fear of showing his discomfort, but once we got in the truck, he let me have it with both barrels in a barrage of yowling cat-profanity that fogged the glass.

That lasted all the way to the vet, where he immediately composed himself. He would never break decorum by showing agitation in front of strangers. He yawned through his exam and accepted his shots with disinterest, never once showing weakness in the face of the enemy or letting on in any way that he was not entirely in control of the situation.

When they expertly brushed the knots out of his flowing, white fur, he extended regally to his full length, as if he considered this to be the deserved treatment of kings such as himself.

Kept it together perfectly. Until we got back in the truck, at which point he resumed his ear-splitting howls all the way home. Back home in front of the dog, he flipped the switch again, calm as ever, casually sniffing the perimeter just to make sure no one had switched houses in his absence.

It all left me a bit nonplused. You expect humans to be two-faced, but a cat? Well, there's nothing to be done, I suppose. With critters, you take what you get. At least there's some comfort in knowing that he has never once tipped over.

Love That Cicada

You will not be reading about cicadas in this space, even though they have become prime grist for every other columnist in America. So spare me your cicada lore.

I don't want to hear about how funny you thought it was that your cat was playing with one in the yard. I don't want to hear how hilarious it is to watch your dog go on a cicada bender, spending his days alternately eating the bugs and throwing them up.

I don't want to hear from you freaks talking about how good they taste cooked in butter with white wine and shallots and tossed with shiitake mushrooms. (Have you ever noticed the "recipes" for undesirables such as insects, slimy plants and hog viscera always call for one part undesirable and a million parts everything else? "Slugs are delicious! Just sauté together a filet mignon, six strips of bacon, a heavy cream sauce and one half of one slug. It's great!")

No, I don't care if you have found the cicadas in your purse, your glovebox or your underpants.

I don't care if they got in the closet and frightened your wife, I don't care if your kids are bashing them with the anti-cicada weapon of choice, the tennis racket.

The cicadas came out of the ground in mid-May, but the hype came out of the ground in March. I haven't seen one yet, and I am already sick of them. Since April, it's been all cicadas all the time. I swear, these insects have better PR operatives than Oprah.

We've been pounded with so much information overkill I feel as if these cicadas are my brothers. I know everything about them there is to know, from their eating habits to the size of their ears.

Mostly it's thanks to these loon college professors and entomologists who have been 30 feet up in a tree since the end of March, making copious notes every time a cicada sheds its skin or picks its proboscis. To them, this is amazing and wonderful. A Christmas that comes once every other decade.

To hear them tell it, you wouldn't think they were bugs, but rather millions and millions of Nicole Kidmans that were crawling up out of the ground. They beg us not to kill them — like there can be any redeeming social value or glamour to a creature that shrieks at the top of its lungs all day, crunches underfoot and primarily ends its life cycle in a cold pool of pet sick.

Supposedly they are already out, although their appearance has been spotty. Some people probably won't get hit too hard, they say — the cicadas can only survive in "soil that hasn't been disturbed for 17 years" like old subdivisions or the path to a Hagerstown weight-loss clinic.

Perhaps the "undisturbed soil" paradigm is why I haven't seen one — ever since we moved in to our home, the dog named Jake Biscuit has made a research project out of digging up every square foot of our yard. (He prefers newly seeded grass, but will make do on "old growth"). In fact, he's probably long since found and devoured every underground cicada larva before they ever got a chance to fatten up.

If he has, that will be the only benefit that dog has ever provided me. And I say this in spite of the efforts of some readers to "educate" me on Jake's behalf — including the anonymous person who mailed me, anthrax style, an unmarked package containing a book by Sharon Creech called "Love That Dog." It contains passages such as:

> *And in the car*
> *he put his head*
> *against my chest*
> *and wrapped his paws*
> *around my arm*
> *as if he were saying*
> *Thank you thank you thank you.*

Nice try, whoever you are, but this is not the way Jake Biscuit conducts his domestic affairs. In my upcoming book, "Hate That Dog," it would be more like:

> *And in the car*
> *he put his head*
> *beneath the brake*
> *and wrapped his paws*
> *around the clutch*
> *as if he were saying*
> *Bet I can make you cause a 17-car pileup on Interstate 81.*

But if he eats all the cicadas on my property all is forgiven — so long as he throws them up on somebody else's.

As with Jake Biscuit, Sometimes Cute is Just Not Worth the Cost

If I haven't written about this sooner, it's been out of guilt. On one hand, I want to close my eyes, ignore it and pretend it never happened. On the other hand, if I do that, someone else might make the same mistake.

Several weeks ago, perhaps you noticed a letter to the editor from a very nice woman named Rosemary Redding who wrote that her family had read about the lawless Jack Russell terrier named Jake Biscuit and decided to obtain a member of the breed for themselves.

I so wish she had contacted me prior to the acquisition so I could have performed a canine intervention.

My first word of advice would have been "NOOOOO!" and if this argument needed to be strengthened, I would have added "NOOOOOOOOO!"

Don't do it. As a rule of thumb, it is good to have a dog that spends more time on the ground than it does in the air.

It is good to have a dog that will sit still every once in a while. I would have settled for 10 minutes a day. It is good to have a dog whose diet does not make a goat look like Morris the Cat. It is good to have a dog that does not view "come," "sit" and "stay" as just suggested behaviors.

One that does not have ADD (Attention Dog Disorder), one whose motto is not chaos, whose philosophy is not "I chew therefore I am," one for whom theft is not a virtue and pranks are not the keys to doggie heaven.

But I was too late.

In a separate letter, Rosemary sent me a photo of their pup Jacob. "We tried to take a Christmas picture, but he grabbed Santa by the throat and dragged him down the stairs," she wrote.

As evidence, sure enough, there is Jacob under the tree with one paw planted firmly on the jolly old elf's throat and his jaws clenched around Santa's dome.

The other shot is equally priceless, showing Jacob (in what doubtless is a rare moment of inaction) staring plaintively at a stuffed snowman on a sled. It's like the animal is savoring the moment before the final attack. Or else thinking, "So many figurines, so little time." Yes, the dogs are cute. I get that. But so was Lizzie Borden. Sometimes cute just isn't worth the cost. Look, I can't tell anyone not to go out and get a Jack Russell. It's just that anyone who is tempted needs to be solidly versed in the facts.

The dogs will slow down, with age, but it didn't happen fast enough for me. They hold onto their pogostickism for years. If you can locate a Jack Russell that is 47 years old, that might be about right.

Jake Biscuit, into his eighth year, was finally starting to figure out that he had slowed down to the point where he had no chance at catching a rabbit or squirrel. (He never was, really, but it took eight years for him to noodle this through.)

So he decided to employ strategy. This was difficult for a dog whose default mechanism was action and whose brain — there is no other way to put this — must be about the size of a walnut. Thinking is not his strength. It is like asking Mike Tyson to conduct a cerebral fight.

So, if he were 40 feet from a squirrel, he (Jake, not Mike Tyson), would slowly commence to stalk a wide circle around the critter. It was a deliberate, measured approach and you could see that the entire time he was immeasurably proud of this cunning technique. Five, 10 minutes he crept in a big, wide arc around the quarry — thinking to himself the entire time, "I am a freaking genius."

Unfortunately, and perhaps the failure was mine for not teaching the animal that the shortest distance between two points is a straight line, he would eventually end up right back where he started, having circled the squirrel completely. And, of course, no closer to the squirrel than he had been at the beginning of the venture.

Clearly, he took this as a massive blow. For the life of him, he could not understand it. All this investment of strategy, time and effort with absolutely no change in circumstance.

It did tend to amuse the squirrel, however, who would watch the entire production out of the corner of its eye with no small degree of interest. It must be a lot like the time I watched "Survivor." I could see what they were doing, but why?

So I am sad to report, Rosemary, that it is unlikely to get better. In fact, there might be worse times to come.

If only I could have reached you sooner. I do apologize.

Mother Nature, It's Not Nice to Fool Jake Biscuit

All right, two words for Mother Nature: Not funny. Everybody's stir crazy. Everybody has a couple of winter-related disasters to relate.

My own personal problem with the winter arose out of garbage. In a rare moment of thaw, about four weeks ago, runoff from the roof bled into the 30-gallon trash can, and that night froze the contents solid. The trash bags have been entombed there ever since.

This has resulted in a sort of an "Ice Man" situation, only with garbage instead of a Neanderthal. I suppose the glacier will spit them out come spring, but for now the only thing I can think to do is ram a stick into it, call it "The Garbagesicle" and sell it as modern art.

But lest we all feel too bad about our circumstances, there is one creature in the Tri-State that has it worse than us, that being our Jack Russell assault weapon known as Jake Biscuit.

Terriers love the land. They sniff it, burrow in it, paw it, caress it and embrace it like few other species. Unfortunately, Jake hasn't seen it in about two months because of all the frozen white stuff that he so despises.

Worse, the snow has hardened to a consistency thicker than the crust on the scrambled eggs on the breakfast bar at 10:59 a.m.

It's something you never stop to think about — that being, how much dogs depend on traction. Not big, long-loping dogs quite so much, but the smaller, higher RPM models.

Jake's legs will whirl to a blur like Wile E Coyote, but he never gets anyplace. For a dog who has grown up thinking he knows something about speed, it is a killer. True story: We took him sledding, and I gathered him in my lap for a ride. I thought he'd freak, but instead he loved it — to feel the wind in his face and finally gain some semblance of motion.

But his day-to-day existence knows no such relief. Even one of his greatest pleasures — his daily evacuation — is of no comfort.

I don't get it, I can't explain it, but he takes an anticipation in the event that is normally reserved for dauphins prior to coronation. About 45 minutes before he's ready, he will strut and preen, calling attention to himself, generally alerting the world that something great is about to transpire.

Once outside, he goes about the task of choosing the right ground with the care and consideration of a French chef choosing just the right truffle. He'll cover two acres looking for just the perfect square foot. Then he'll hunch, throw his ears back, raise his nose to the heavens and commence.

But on the ice, it is trickier. First, the snows cover the scents, so he has trouble sniffing out ground that is worthy enough for his daily blessing. And on one unfortunate day, he settled on land that possessed just a little too much slope.

He settled into position OK, but mid-ceremony he began to lose purchase on the ice-capped snow and slide ever so slowly down the hill. Once initiated, there was no question of stopping the procedure, so this wasn't an option. I guess to a terrier it's bad luck, or something.

There was nothing he could do as he began to pick up speed and, horrors!, spiral a lazy 360 degrees on the ice. To his credit, he held form. As he slid, he never once broke his pose, looking like a piece of statuary that someone had cut loose from the top of a ski jump.

The look of mournful indignity on his face all the while would break the heart.

He gradually slowed to a stop, but the damage had been done. Normally, on completion he will proudly paw at the ground like a race horse, sending dirt and blades of grass skyward as he demands the world acknowledge his heroism for what he has just accomplished.

He did try, but it was a failure. On his second swipe he once again got no traction, his front legs went out from under him and he came down hard on his snout.

The deed was done, but he was a changed dog. Instead of sprinting back to the house for his treat, he just kind of dragged along, his head low in depression. In all, what was normally his most glorious time of day had been rendered to no better than a B-minus.

Spring can't come soon enough for Jake Biscuit.

A Breed Apart

If I can do no other good in this world than to steer you away from the breed of dog known as the Jack Russell terrier, my life will have been a success. They are bad dogs. Very bad dogs.

I don't know who this Jack Russell chap was, but with hindsight I doubt he would have leant his own name to the breed. He might instead have called it the Al Sharpton terrier or the Bill O'Reilly terrier.

This is because Jack Russells are 17 pound dogs who imagine themselves to be 250 and capable of whipping anyone in the barroom.

Take our dog Jake Biscuit. Please.

To my knowledge, Jake has never started a fight that he's won, but he only views his defeats as encouragement and motivation for the next fray no matter how large or malodorous his opponent may be.

Or small, for that matter. He went screaming after a cat recently intent on shredding it — until the cat took the fiendishly clever defensive move of just standing there and looking at him. Jake slammed on the brakes about 10 feet from the cat, obviously having failed to draw up the next phase of his battle plan after the charge.

It is his custom to boss everyone on the entire block around and when the cat failed to comply with his order to turn tail and run, he was baffled.

If kitties were the most dangerous form of wildlife on our property, I suppose this would not be a problem.

But it was close to midnight the other evening, when he demanded to go outside and give the premises one last inspection before retiring.

Ears, nose and tail all pointed to the heavens, he grandly gave the place a once-over, making sure he was the king of all he surveyed.

And that's when he first saw the skunk.

It was a big one, not that it would have mattered to Jake one way or the other. His feet spun madly in the air before he ever started to move, much like the Road Runner in the old cartoons.

Never mind that he had failed to achieve success in confrontations against any dog, cat, coon, groundhog, mole, rat, vole or opossum. This time it would be different. And he was right about that. It was different, though not in any positive way.

He's a fast dog, and he crossed the lot in three jumps exactly, barking, braying, howling, shrieking and otherwise announcing his arrival in ways that gave his enemy plenty of time to prepare.

Being the black of night, there was no seeing what happened, although a couple of remaining senses filled in the gaps. In a second, Jake's throatal cacophony ceased and the neighborhood grew deathly quiet.

Then a fragrance gathered out over the yard. It started out low and then started to grow. Neighbors began slamming their windows shut.

Then the baffled dog himself returned from the sortie, pawing at his eyes and, in a word, reeking.

Naturally, he did not blame himself. He was only forced to retreat because his enemy possessed a poison gas, a weapon of mass destruction not sanctioned under the Geneva Convention. If anything, he blamed us for not having "inspectors on the ground," i.e., we weren't letting him out often enough.

Fortunately for the dog, I was asleep during the affair. I am certain that had I not been, our household would have awoken in the morning with one dog-dish too many.

Multiple baths have made no difference, and the scent is now all through the house. Our roommate tried burning one of those exotic, far-eastern incenses and I guess it's supposed to be a pleasing smell, but all things considered I sort of prefer skunk.

We've been told tomato juice works, but the thought of a tomato-dog-skunk brew is equally unappealing.

The only one happy over the whole affair is Jake, who is thrilled because he no longer smells like himself. This is very important to a dog for some reason, and he's re-marking the entire neighborhood, sort of like a "Guess who?" calling card to other dogs.

The experience has left me feeling dismally like the mailman in Marmaduke, who once pointed the animal out to his substitute and said "He doesn't bite, but oohhh brother..."

Buttering Up the In-Laws' Dog

Being on my own for so many years, my idea of Thanksgiving had always been to put a slice of pumpkin on my Slim Jims.

But now things are different and on the holiday I not only found myself surrounded by people, but actually helped cook. This was frightening business.

Fortunately, a famous chef once told me the age-old secret to successful cooking: Add butter. If you're out of butter, add bacon.

Yup, that's about it. Turkey drying out? Add butter. Sweet potatoes not everybody's favorite vegetable? Add butter. Stuffing sort of bland? Add butter. Iced tea too weak? Add butter.

I didn't even get a turkey this year. I just got a 20-pound block of butter and chain sawed it bird-shaped. Then I stuffed it with butter.

Everything was perfectly under control and we were feeling good about the timetable. As a matter of fact, everything was going so well I made the serious error of deciding I could take the visiting dog Crosby for a brief stroll.

Crosby is in-laws' Kris and Brad's beautiful chocolate lab, who despite being still mostly puppy, has grown roughly to the size of a furry aircraft carrier with a head like a landing strip, only wider. Personality-wise, he is kind of like Warren Zevon's "Excitable Boy."

That morning I had made the twin errors of leaving the bedroom door ajar and sleeping atop the covers. I was awakened by a Very Cold Nose on the rear, which I must say, is information I should pass along to the Seth Thomas corporation, since this was more fully effective than about five alarm clocks bundled together.

So, being up a little earlier than intended, it seemed logical to take the huge dog and our small dog Jake Biscuit for a little morning romp in the back yard.

Unfortunately, I was lacking some key information, that being that Crosby takes directions worse than Alec Baldwin. The idea of a morning romp was fine with him, but apparently he found the backyard a little too artistically confining. He stuck around for about 2.1 seconds before bolting off in long, loping strides that carried about one city block per jump.

The ensuing chase was complicated by the fact that a jailbreak sounded good to Jake Biscuit as well, so I had to alternately chase after Crosby and then turn and chase Jake back to the house. Of course, the dogs were low to the ground and beneath neighborhood hedge levels, so if anyone happened to look out the window at that particular time they would have seen only some crazed man running 80 feet forward, then 60 feet back, then 80 forward, 60 back, 80 forward, 60 back and they might have had some trouble making sense of it.

Crosby was about 10 blocks away by this time, and all I could do was stay relatively close and hope for some unforeseen development that would let me collar him. He was having great fun, of course - letting me get within about a millimeter of his collar before bounding another three miles into the hinterlands.

Then I noticed something. It was almost as if there was an invisible tether between us. If I moved in his direction, he'd run away, but conversely he would come nearer when I moved back. Thus the game entered Phase II. This involved me sprinting back toward the house at full speed through everybody's back yard, with him in hot pursuit. It was so simple, but it was working beautifully.

And that's when he saw the other dog.

I'd been running like an idiot, not noticing that he had long since stopped, his attention distracted by another lab penned in a back yard. At first there was much sniffing, followed up by much braying. That was followed up by much hissing — coming from me, mostly, as I tried to get the two clowns to shut up before the home's owner came out in his nightshirt with a shotgun and dispatched us all to that great "I Love Lucy" show in the sky.

Just when all seemed lost, my mother-in-law Kay came to the rescue, bagging Crosby just as neat as you please. All it took to weaken his constitution was a dog biscuit — which I am sure contains a high percentage of butter.

Of Mice and Men, the Mice Get More Slack with Women

When the cat named Colonel Sanders showed up under our porch with an attitude and an appetite the size of Kansas, I quickly realized I was beat.

Despite my misgivings about adding another life form to the asylum, the women of the house were cooing the asbestos off the shingles, so there I was, left alone with nothing to hold onto but my rationalizations.

Since we live in a house that gives the Pyramids a run for their longevity, the structure is not exactly what you would call air tight. Hang gliders routinely call us and ask if they can ride the drafts that come through the ancient windows, and until we replaced the doors a full-grown leopard could have walked in through the cracks.

When we moved in, we had to go through a lengthy screening process with the mice, who weren't particularly keen on sharing the premises and wanted to be sure they were getting solid housemates.

Since then it's been a war of attrition, with my arsenal of surface-to-surface, anti-mouse weaponry meeting with varying amounts of success.

If you are a guy who has ever had to deal with a family of mice on one hand, and a family of females on the other, you already know the problem. The women want the mice GONE and they want them gone YESTERDAY and they want you to exhaust ALL METHODS of mouse eradication NO MATTER WHAT the consequences.

Except they don't want you to hurt them.

This essentially gives them carte blanche to defiantly raise up on their little hind feet (the mice, not the women) and thumb their claws at you because they know you are hamstrung.

For example, you are not allowed to employ any device that will cause the mouse to squeal. They don't want to be blow drying their hair and putting on their lipstick (the women, not the mice) in the morning to the sound of "eeeeeeeeee!"

This rules out snap traps and those awful little sticky sheets that catch the mouse like a sheet of flypaper, and make even me oogy.

Using poison is sketchy because we have a dog. So I didn't know exactly how to kill the mice without, you know, killing them.

Enter the cat, which I hoped, at least, would be a remorseless killing machine.

Perhaps you've noticed, in the animal kingdom hierarchy, the *felis domesticus* can get away with a lot more than the *husbandis bossedaroundius*.

I mean look, if it were up to me, I would use a few little moussie night-night pellets, tell him thanks for the memories, then watch him leave the house in search of water until his liver exploded. Total time of mouse discomfort: 3.2 seconds. A cat, on the other hand, will torture the poor little thing for hours, tearing off its limbs one by one as it writhes in pain and terror (I assume) while the cat plays the "Oh no, it's getting away; oh no it's not" game.

But to a woman, a cat can get away with this because "It's what he does."

Um. Hm. Next time she catches you downtown drinking with another woman, try "But it's what I do" as an excuse and see how it plays then. Cats, you will see, get breaks than men do not.

So I agreed to take in the colonel, partly on the assumption that at least he would keep the mouse population at bay — although to be honest, by this time I had done most of the "heavy lifting" on the matter, which had become pretty much resolved in my favor through methods that are best left undescribed, just in case the EPA is reading.

A year later, however, I am happy to report that the cat has made his first kill. I caught him in the basement out of the corner of my eye doing the ritualistic pounce, bat, watch, repeat. So absorbed was he with this new recreation that a thermonuclear device could have gone off in the catbox and it wouldn't have phased him.

I gave the cat a half hour or so of playing time, before I figured I better go sweep up the remains before the parts became too scattered. I walked over to the animal and said, "What you got there, boycat?" The spell broken, he looked up from where he had been batting around his — cricket.

The Great White Hunter had bagged a stupid insect, and he was acting for all the world as if he'd just killed a woolly mammoth with an olive fork.

He has since added a moth to the trophy case. I'm sure the cat would want you to know that this required special skills, seeing as how this game operated on vertical planes as well as horizontal. Although it about gave him a heart attack when his catch, instead of going left or right, went up.

All in all, it was a pretty pathetic effort. I hope no mice were watching.

Cloning Pets is Ludicrous

All I could think of was the Stephen King novel "Pet Sematary." A cat gets pancaked on the highway, distressing the little girl who owned it. So the old coot next door discloses to the girl's pop the location of a secret place where, if you bury a dead animal, it will come back to life the next day.

The upside of this comeback is that the creature is alive; the downside is that it's evil. In that respect, it kind of parallels the career of Joan Rivers.

And it also somewhat parallels the situation in Texas, where a woman identified only as "Julie" paid $50,000 to have her dead cat cloned. The cat, named Nicky, had been her companion for 17 years and she wanted another just like it.

So scientists with the San Francisco lab Genetic Savings and Clone took a chunk of hide (Nicky's, not Julie's) and cooked up an identical kitten, which was dutifully named "Little Nicky."

Little Nicky is not only the spitting image of Dead Nicky, but the interested parties all report that it bears many of the same personality traits. For example, the ex-cat liked food and, remarkably enough, so does the copy cat.

Hey, if Julie is happy, I'm happy. But a couple of things strike me as odd about these Frankenfelines. First of all, this lab that calls itself Genetic Savings and Clone — if you're a company that deals with life and death I'm not sure it's a good idea to give yourself a cutesy name like that.

It's fine for a hair stylist to call itself Shear Terror or The Exscissorcist or something, but a genetic laboratory? That's like owning a funeral home down by the harbor and calling it the Marine Corpse.

Then there's the whole "playing God" debate, and the "where do you draw the line on cloning" debate and the "70 million cats in shelters need good homes" debate, all of which I'll take a pass on.

Although I will say, if I'm Julie's husband I'm nervous. First sign of a gray hair and development of a slight paunch, and she's propped up on her elbow one night in bed, just staring at you.

"Um, what is it dear?"

"Oh nothing. I was just thinking about how much I love you — and could I get a little scraping from the roof of your mouth?"

But the issue I can't overlook is this: $50,000 — is she CRAZY?

I own a cat. I love cats. I am not going to pay 50 grand for an animal that, when it comes right down to it, is going to pretty much resemble and act like every other cat that has been around since they were domesticated by the ancient Egyptians.

First, you can always find a cat that looks like your old cat. And spare me this whole "personality" argument. Look, my cat, Colonel Sanders, has a few personality traits that make him a Little Bit Different from other cats. For example, he doesn't like to hunt mice. But that doesn't make him Tony Kornheiser. He's not going to be doing standup in the Village anytime soon, or commenting on popular vote vis a vis the Electoral College.

He's a cat.

A great cat, a beautiful cat, but a cat. And sorry, but if I have a choice between a BMW M3 and a cat that looks just like him, but isn't — well, you might as well pass me the key fob right now.

It's like that ad with the guy who agonizes whether he should have bought a Harley-Davidson motorcycle or a dinette set. "Beachfront property/cat. Beachfront property/cat. Went with the cat."

True, I don't know how you put a price on a beloved animal, but I do know that $50,000 ain't it. Especially when it isn't the beloved animal at all, but a different one. Just pray that Julie's kids don't own any goldfish. She could find herself with "Little Goldie," "Little, Little

77

Goldie," "Little, Little, Little Goldie" and be a quarter of a million dollars lighter in the space of a week.

Meanwhile, Genetic Savings and Clone says that nine more of these cats are "in production," six of which have been ordered and three of which are going to be used as "showroom models." Since the company is into clever names, we can bet the showroom models will have monikers like "Ford Feline," "Catillac" and "Mazda Meowta." When you're creating life, there's no such thing as being too cute.

Turns Out Cat Lady Had Little Nicky Cloned for Science

I had just popped a couple of Vioxx to ease the pain in my Celebrex when the phone rang. It was a woman at work telling me to call the Cat Lady.

Like most average Americans of my age and gender, I had no idea what that meant.

"Julie — the woman you wrote about who cloned the cat," she said. "I just talked to her and she wants you to give her a call."

"Oh, OK, good one. Ha ha. Now what do you want?"

"No, seriously, I have her cell phone number right here."

"Right, right. Well, see, the thing about that is, I already have Katharine Hepburn on hold and I have to get back to Gwyneth Paltrow right after I talk to her and I've been keeping Sharon Stone waiting since forever, so I couldn't possibly ..."

"I'm serious. Julie says there were some inaccuracies in the wire reports that she wants to clear up."

Instinctively, I immediately knew two things: 1.) She wasn't kidding; 2.) The woman, a cat lover herself, had already taken Julie's side. In fact, they had already struck up a rapport. She had nothing but glowing things to say about Julie, the woman who gained fame last week when it came to light she had paid $50,000 for a clone of her cat Nicky.

It was one of those few times you will not hear me praising Al Gore for inventing the Internet, because it has become too easy for people across this great land to read things that were never intended to be spread west of Little Orleans.

I can't tell you how many times I've been in the position of having to tell someone unfamiliar with this column that I don't meeeaan nuthin' — all thanks to http protocol.

It was a difficult decision whether to call back, but at least I figured I'd get 30 minutes on how "cats are people, too" and how she can communicate with animals through a mutual twitching of their ears. You know, good bizarre material for future columns.

Imagine the crushing disappointment when she answered the phone and turned out to be normal — more a woman of science than anything.

Her father was a doctor, and had argued some time ago that cloning was a valid science which, 20 years down the road, would be considered mainstream. Julie said she was skeptical, but curious nevertheless.

Unlike most press accounts had it, she did not have Little Nicky cloned out of grief for Big Nicky; the cloning plan had been more than two years in the making. On the issue of cost, she said $50,000 indeed may seem expensive, but noted it was a choice she made — rather than replace her aging car, in this instance. Plus, she gives more than that to charity, including no-kill animal shelters.

Besides, she asked, would you really rather have a BMW or your cat?

I cast an uneasy glance over at Colonel Sanders, who had chosen that particular moment to contentedly chew the cover off of one of my leatherbound Tolstoy classics. I don't believe animals can understand what you're saying, but, well, he was within earshot, so I tentatively answered, "The cat?" Neither Julie nor the Colonel want to know what I was really thinking at that point.

Julie continued that she had never intended to go public. She changed course when the cloned cat turned out to be startlingly similar to the ex-cat in personality. Neither cat, for example, has the traditional feline hatred of water. Both are happy to jump in the shower.

"It's uncanny; it's not like a new cat, it's like an extension of the old cat."

This could yield some important clues, Julie said, to the age-old nature-vs.-nurture debate. It appears to her that we might be born with a personality and behavior that is less influenced by the environment as we are led to believe.

At this point I had to interrupt. "You mean to tell me that all you want to talk about is rational science? Do you realize that does me no good whatsoever? I'm a humor writer, give me something I can use. Tell me how the ghost of Big Nicky appears to you every night and whispers winning lottery numbers into your ear. Tell me that Little Nicky knows something only Big Nicky could have known, like his AOL password, or something. Come on, say something wacky. And would it kill you to shriek a little?"

But it was of no use. She was determined to be calm, friendly and reasoned. At the end of a half hour, it became clear that we simply were not communicating on the same level. Or maybe we were. After all, I couldn't see her. Maybe she was twitching her ears.

Now Everyday is Groundhog Day

For years I've felt as if it were me against the world. Or to be more accurate, me against the world of the groundhog.

I've been on an island; no one else cares. Or if they care, they take the side of the groundhog because they are, and this is a direct quote: "Cute."

Bah. Once again this summer I've watched my beautiful garden turn into the woodchucks' own personal silo, but I've got to live with this because they are cute. I put forth the postulate that Ted Bundy was "cute." I began to draw parallels to the necessity of execution.

"Listen, Andrea..." I said. She didn't, of course. No woman ever does.

Instead she went off on a diatribe about if I were to attempt to use poison, the next dose would be for myself. I locked myself in my lonely writers' garret and commenced feeling sorry for myself.

If I only had one ally in this fight, I thought, just one living entity that saw things my way, that saw groundhogs for the flowerbed leveling entity they are. If I only had one friend who would pursue these creatures as ruthlessly as myself.

Now I have found one. Now I wish I hadn't.

Enter the Jack Russell terrier named Jake Biscuit.

I was sitting on the back porch when I saw one of these lawless creatures sauntering through the yard just as careless and joyful and carefree as if he were posing for a painting by Renoir on the banks of the Seine.

Suddenly I had an idea. The Grinch had a wonderful, awful idea. I called the dog. Jake loves to be outside, so he went sprinting out full bore into the yard gaining Concorde-like speed with each stride until he was only a brown and white blaze too fast for anything but the most sophisticated of radar.

Unfortunately, Columbo, he's not. He shot past the groundhog, leaving the creature's fur blowing in the backdraft.

I sighed and went to retrieve him, pulling him back by his harness while he pulled in the other direction with the force of many men. I pointed, but he just looked at my hand, thinking there might be a ball in it.

The groundhog, meanwhile, was watching the whole spectacle with a quizzical, mildly interested expression like a supermarket attendant might watch someone with a load of groceries trying to get their cart up over the curb.

All of a sudden the Alpo must have triggered the right mechanism in that tiny little brain of his, for Jake saw the animal, and then all bets were off. He wheeled a 180 and put forth a burst that would have embarrassed War Emblem.

The woodchuck, which had been strolling along, suddenly developed a livelier interest in his journey and the ensuing chase was truly something to watch. To Jake's advantage was speed; the groundhog's advantage was a nearby burrow into which he fit but the dog didn't quite.

Most of Jake fit, but his rear end, which is roughly the size of John Goodman's, did not.

Jake lodged himself in the hole and we haven't seen much of anything of him but his tail since.

Having failed at penetration, Jake turned his attention to excavation. For the next 40 minutes dirt shot up out of the ground like a rooster.

Since that time, however, he has had no other thought but to get that rodent.

Open the door and he shoots to the groundhog hole to resume his archaeology. He has forgotten everything — all other reasons to be outside, like doing his business or chasing his ball.

My idea is that his brain is so small there's only room for one idea in it a time, so all other pursuits fall by the wayside.

Some would say it's not Jake's fault, it's they way they are bred. He's been genetically trained to burrow, so that instinct overrides all others.

Well, maybe so, but if that's the case I would argue that this selective dog breeding has gone way too far.

Bucky the Deer Takes His Paws from the Cold

There's nothing I love more than a good deer story, so I was fascinated to read this week about Bucky, a young animal that was rescued from traffic by Starla and Kevin Hall of Hagerstown.

In a few brief days, the deer has become something of a pet, and the Halls are hoping to find someone to care for Bucky and give it medical attention.

Of course, Maryland being Maryland, there are about 75,926 laws on the books dealing with folks who happen to have a deer on their porch. But happily, state officials seem to be working on a satisfactory solution that won't involve deer bologna.

Kevin said they took the deer in because it was in traffic near Godlove's Liquors (when is the Godlove family going to open a lingerie store? It can't happen soon enough for me) and appeared to be "confused." OK, confused, fair enough. But speaking from my own personal experience, I do not believe I have ever seen a deer that appeared to have a plan.

Deer, to me, always look as if they have just at that very moment been beamed down from Mars. Organization does not appear to be a strength.

Although Bucky — if it had been a girl what do they name it, Jane Doe? — does seem to possess some rather extraordinary powers.

The first night in its new home, the deer managed to open the porch door and return to the wild and, more incredibly, later that night it returned and let itself back in.

"He got in and out and we haven't figured out (how) yet," said Starla.

There have to be about 10 billion dogs around the world that have to be amazingly steamed right about now. For five centuries, dogs everywhere have struggle unsuccessfully to understand doorknob technology, and here some stupid fawn strolls in and gets it on the first stab.

Must be some critter. If I'm the Halls, first thing I do is padlock the fridge. Already, they say Bucky is much like a dog, in that it follows them around and enjoys being petted. Again, he has it down. All the perks of being a dog, without having to stoop to the indignity of learning to fetch.

Wildlife officials, of course, frown on making a deer too comfortable around the house, because it becomes all the harder for the animal to return and survive in the natural kingdom.

The deer becomes comfortable around humans and pretty soon he's expecting handouts, losing natural instincts, watching the morning talk shows, playing Xbox and generally forgetting what it's like to eat a cold shrub on a foggy morning.

I wish I could help the Halls in their admirable attempt to find the poor creature a good home — I suppose I could offer to take it up to my folks' place in Berkeley Springs.

They already have a dozen or so, one more would hardly be noticed. Technically they are not pets, although they might as well be. My brother-in-law was looking for a place to hunt over Thanksgiving, and I said he could use our place.

The benefit is that it would save the expense of ammunition. These deer are so tame, all it would take would be to hit them over the coconut with the stock.

No, tame isn't the word. They're more aggressive than that — always knocking on the door and demanding to know why no new rhododendrons have been set out for them to nibble, or crossly reminding the family that "the azaleas are getting tough" and lobbying for fresh shoots.

Last election, I think a couple of them were even caught trying to vote. But keep in mind, I heard that secondhand.

So I hope the Halls can find a suitable situation for Bucky, and that it happens in a timely fashion. After all, the message from the naturalists is a chilling one: The more time you spend around the human race, the less chance you have.

Bucky Dominated the News Like Only Animals Can

Well, at least we know what sells in Western Maryland — sex and deer. National press descended on the region twice last week, once to chronicle the release of a prostitution ring's "Black Book" in Frederick, and also to follow the plight of a deer named Bucky which was taken in by a local family intent on saving its life.

The deer made out the better of the two.

At least it was more of a feel-good story. Staggering dazed and confused along a highway, it was saved and eventually released into the wild, just barely escaping the hands of the Maryland Department of Natural "Dick Dastardly" Resources, which wanted the animal killed and tested for something called "chronic wasting disease."

Oh, come on. Chronic wasting disease? That's the best they could do? The state could have at least said the deer might have contracted rabies, or mad deer disease, or whooping cough — or just about anything.

But chronic wasting disease? That sounds like something a junior high kid would come up with for his note to the teacher after feigning illness to go to the ole fishing hole.

"Dear Ms. Fussbudget,

"Please excuse Mitch from school yesterday. He had chronic wasting disease.

Thank you,

Mitch's mom."

This story was so big the "Today" show was here, the governor was notified and a news chopper was hovering overhead. A helicopter. When did we turn into L.A.? What, did they mistake Eastern Boulevard for Interstate 5?

This was a deer, for heaven's sake, not the Beltway sniper.

So the DNR wanted to kill the deer. By the end of the day, I wanted to kill the deer. What there was in people's thought processes that made them say to themselves, "Hey, a deer is in trouble; I better call Tim Rowland" I cannot even begin to say. But if I took one call on the topic, I took 30.

By the end of Thursday, I hated that deer like I have hated no non-office-holding creature in God's creation. One very kind gentleman offered to pay me personally $100 if I could facilitate the deer's freedom. This caused an awful moral dilemma, since by that time I was privy to the information that Bucky, if that is his real name, had already been freed.

I got calls from People for the Ethical Treatment of Animals. I got calls from family members of People for the Ethical Treatment of Animals and from the father of a man who lives in southeastern Virginia, where People for the Ethical Treatment of Animals is headquartered.

I got phone calls from children. I got phone calls from people who run game preserves and from people who knew people who run game preserves. I got a call from someone who offered to transport the deer across state lines to West Virginia, where it could be kept nii-iice and legal.

I got a call from a woman who was talking so fast I couldn't understand a word that she said.

Finally I snapped. "This is The Herald-freaking-Mail, not 'Field and Stream!'" I shouted. "I cannot save that deer and even if I could, I wouldn't. Besides, you don't know that deer. All you know is that it's fluffy. Maybe it has bad intent, you don't know. It could be cute, but obnoxious, like Paris Hilton."

By the end of the day, I was entirely beaten down. All I could rasp into the phone was a weak, "I'll see what I can do. Thank you for calling."

The only people who had a worse day than me had to be the DNR. They did their jobs and did everything by the book, and because of that a lot of people wanted to string them up. Truth be told, it was one of those times when "regulations" might have best been overlooked, but if your boss is the state government, try explaining to an Annapolis bureaucrat that you felt the need to inject a little common sense into the situation.

Great Deer Chase Could Give Mummers a Run for Their Money

Forget the Mummers Parade. It's over; it's history. It had its day, but now it's only attracting a tenth of the crowd it once did. It's sooo 1973.

I'm not recommending that we throw it on the parade scrap heap, however. It is just that the Mummers needs a makeover to reinvigorate itself, and happily this week we were handed an idea for exactly how this can be done.

Flash forward to Monday morning when two deer raided the downtown, leading police on a merry chase before becoming wedged between a wall and an oil tank behind the Presbyterian Church of

Hagerstown. I've heard of a steeplechase, but this is ridiculous. Or maybe they were praying for their souls for eating my tomatoes.

Police had been hoping to drive the animals toward City Park, since they were in danger of becoming hood ornaments for oncoming traffic.

But the deer had other ideas, perhaps thinking that one sanctuary was the same as another, whether or not it had the word "wildlife" in front of it.

That, or they were two months early for the nativity scene.

Outside of that, the history of deer in the Bible is notably scarce. "Doe unto others as ..." No.

I don't know if the Chamber of Commerce considers this a win or not. They're always wanting more foot traffic downtown. And if the Hagerstown Suns were still playing, you know they'd count the deer toward their nightly attendance totals.

But that aside, you wouldn't figure on deer to be much of a benefit to the city — although if venison is on the menu at Duffy's this weekend I, for one, will be suspicious.

Listening to the scanner, for one terrible second, I thought this could become another Bucky situation.

Can you believe it's been four long years since Bucky was rescued from traffic and became America's Deer after the DNR tried to send it to that great salt lick in the sky?

This episode had a semi-happier ending, primarily because it didn't drag on for six weeks. We got them out of town faster than a Burmese refugee. The deer darted into the tranquility of the church and then were darted with a shot of tranquilizer from thou holy air rifle.

They were then dutifully transported to the wildlife area at Indian Springs, where one of them died anyway. Oh well, we tried. Seems kind of ungrateful on the part of the deer, but what are you going to do?

It's like Mozart the Meerkat — give an animal a starring role and this is how you are repaid.

Unfortunately, to my knowledge, we never had the time to name this poor critter, which would have lent the tragic story more poignancy. She's just another faceless Jane Doe.

But to return to my original point, I think we should posthumously name her "Mummer."

I think you see where I am going with this.

The city of Pamplona in Spain has made a killing off the annual Running of the Bulls and I think we could transition rather smoothly from the Mummers Parade to the Running of the Deer — or as we could call it, "Mummer's Parade." In honor of the late Mummer the Deer.

What would happen if we turned 1,500 deer loose in the middle of downtown Hagerstown? I don' know, but I know for an absolute fact that I would be willing to pay to find out.

And I bet a lot of other people would too. Face it, deer make everything more interesting. And certainly there is no shortage of the commodity around here.

Yes, PETA may object on the grounds that they object to everything, but that only increases the publicity. And just wait until they find out that the grand marshal of the First Annual Running of the Deer is Michael Vick.

Cruel? No more so than these varmints eating my tomatoes.

Animal Tracking System Takes Counting Sheep, Cows to New Level

A friend just got a new puppy. It's a rottweiler. It makes me nervous. Not because it's a rottweiler, but because it came pre-installed with a computer chip.

Now I know what you're thinking: There he goes again, about to take some harmless, and even beneficial program and blow it entirely out of all meaningful proportion.

You would be correct.

But I don't care what you think, because I am deeply concerned about this trend toward computerizing animals, under the auspices of making them "easier to find." Um hm. Easier to find — and program, I'd say. All of a sudden Dave Barry's joke about dogs receiving their signals from a "dog satellite" takes on a frightening plausibility.

And it's not just pets, it's happening with farm animals, too, according to an eye-opening story in the April 23 Herald-Mail.

The U.S. National Animal Identification System, the paper says, will centrally assign each farm with a unique seven-character identification number and then each individual animal will receive a special 15-digit number and (keep in mind, the party of "small government" is currently in power) animals that are part of group will receive a 13-character number.

Whew. Better hope cows are good at math.

Every time a calf is born, I guess you have to call the government. "Hello, Department of Agriculture? This is farmer 853D36H, and I'd like to report that cow No. 936502562935957 has just had a calf, that would be by bull No. 046205673850936, out of group 4962950169462 and we'd like to name it No. 595395103497249. That's my Social Security number squared, so it's kind of special. What? Yes, I'll hold. That number's taken? Well what about No. 3759 ... Wait a sec. What's that Mildred? She had twins?"

Farmer won't need a veterinarian, he'll need a numerologist.

And it's not just cows. The program also applies to "farmers who have cattle, bison, llamas, alpacas, deer, elk, horses, goats, poultry, sheep and pigs." So I guess if you're a monkey farmer, you're off the hook.

But not if you're an aquafarmer. Oh no. You will have to register "certain species of fish, as well as mussels, scallops, oysters and crawfish."

Animals will be identified by tags, including computer microchips and radio transmitters that enable the government to track them by satellite. That's the job I want: Monitoring seafood activity.

Operator One: Sparrow to Mother Goose, Sparrow to Mother Goose, we have a situation here. Mussel No. 358935629456398 is making a break for it.

Operator Two: Roger that, activating tactical antimussel missile.

Operator One: Tracking mussel missile. Negative that Mother Goose, mussel missile missed mussel. But it leveled Chincoteague.

Makes you wonder how much easier Noah's job would have been had he been armed with modern technology. The unicorns might be with us today if only they'd been afforded a computer chip. On the down side, I don't know how you go about computerizing an oyster.

It will just give those snooty waiters across the country one more thing to brag about on the menu. "Yes sir, an excellent choice, this oyster is from Breton Sound, Louisiana. It is salty with a sweet aftertaste, tender, but with a bite to the tooth — and it has 256 megs of RAM."

So why are we doing all this? Why are we going to the time, trouble and expense of a massive national animal inventory?

Terrorists, of course.

Program literature states that "The Sept. 11, 2001, attacks make it clear that an intentional introduction of an animal disease is a real risk."

Begging the government's pardon, but I for one don't see how this is very clear at all. Somebody's going to hijack a chicken and fly it into a KFC? Are terrorists breeding a fearsome new strain of suicide cows?

And I'll be honest, I just don't come in contact with an alpaca all that often.* It's been a long time since I've pushed away from the dinner table and said, "Ummm, that was some gooood alpaca."

* By sheer coincidence, as of 2008 I own four alpacas. Who could have known?

Big Deer Contest Cannot Replace Checking Stations

It's a good thing that the 2006 session of the Maryland General Assembly is about to commence, because the wheels are clearly coming off state government, and only swift action by our lawmakers can correct the listing ship.

Last year's twin crises of medical malpractice and slot machine legalization look like mere child's play next to this year's issues of deer-checking stations and jailhouse cola.

People frequently ask, "Tim, do you ever tire of being ahead of the curve all the time?" and I have to honestly respond, "Yes, yes I do." For example, I was a lone voice of warning in the wilderness when the state first began to talk about "automated deer checking."

I'm sure people ignored Noah, too, but you would think that a man of my track record would have some tree-cred when he sensed a forest-related catastrophe. The problem, in this case, arose when the state determined there wasn't any real need to take your kill to a local checking station for processing. It could be done over the phone, or even online.

Any country boy is going to see about a dozen things wrong with this picture. First, you can't eliminate the traditional check-in of the deer. It's sort of a pick up truck version of the blessing of the hounds. Deer season and checking station go together like fundraiser and silent auction.

I'm sure you have seen one, even if you did not recognize it for what it was. At first blush, a checking station appears to be a quaint little grocery/convenience store with a couple of gas pumps outside in a gravel lot. Well, gravel if the owners are pretentious.

Ever since the dawn of deer and state regulations, man has gone into the forest, blown away Bambi and then hauled the corpse to the checking station to be recorded for all time in the annals of state government. We cannot tell you how many children are starving on the streets of Baltimore ghettos, but we can tell you whether the deer kill was up in Allegany County for the month of November 1996.

(This process is peculiar to deer, I think. I don't know for sure, but I've never heard of anyone having to check a squirrel.)

You generally can tell you are at a deer checking station if: 1.) They seem to have an excessive inventory of Hostess Fruit Pies; 2.) They have a wood stove (usually); and 3.) There is a copious amount of cork bulletin board space choked with fading Polaroid pictures of dead animals.

Many of these stores have built on additional rooms to hold all the lies that are told around the wood stove concerning "near misses" of bucks that have more points than LeBron James. It's a chance to swap stories, get the family together to have their smiling photo taken in front of some furry bleeding thing, eat a bologna sub, drink some beer, spit, and be truly sociable.

I am in no way being facetious when I tell you that a morning at a checking station is a good and wonderfully entertaining time. It's a great part of country life.

So naturally, the state is — would it be trite if I said "gutting" the program? Those little checking stores depended on the extra cash (mostly generated through the sale of Hostess Fruit Pies) that the deer-checking traffic brought in.

The state, for its part has indicated it may try a new and innovative approach to boost sales at former checking stations, specifically — and I wish I were kidding about this, but I am not — a "biggest deer contest."

Hey look, it's what happens when a bunch of bureaucrats laid off by the state lottery commission get picked up by the DNR. Pretty soon they're going to tattoo six pieces of fruit on the deer's hide and if you scratch the fur off three lemons, you win a prize.

But I mourn for the hunter. What's the fun of bagging a buck if you can't sit around the checking station talking about it all day, while the venison slowly decays to a liquidy pulp to the sounds of Toby Keith? Instead, you've got to sit alone in the cold blue light of your computer screen as you try to log on to register the dead animal. That's not what we know and love about hunting.

Can you imagine Buffalo Bill trying to Google his hunting license as a PDF? The greatest hunter the young nation ever saw might have been lost for wont of Adobe Acrobat, Version 6.0. To me, it's a sad, sad day when you ask a hunter about a T-1 and he doesn't know if you're talking about a rifle or a broadband connection.

It is an equally sad day when I ramble on for 20 inches and forget to weigh in on what was supposed to be an equal mainstay in this column, the issue of jailhouse cola, which I referred to in Paragraph 2. But corrections officers be assured, I'll get to it at some point. I'll have time. Unfortunately for everyone, it's going to be a long, long, legislative session.

The Geese at Fort Ritchie Had Better Duck, Duck

Since its closure, the former Fort Ritchie base known now as PenMar has always resembled a Hannah-Barbera cartoon, so I suppose it was just a matter of time until it got laid low by critters.

Geese, specifically. Ducks would have been better, but hey, I have to work with what they give me.

PenMar Executive Director Rich Rook says up to 800 geese at a time like to chill at base's lakes, and that their leavins' can amount to a pound and a half each per day.

So the PenMar board voted (who says they are incapable of making a decision) to give Rook the authority to call the Geese Police to "discourage" the birds from setting up camp. You know how it works. Goose gets a visit in the middle of the night from a hired goon, who threatens — threatens what? It's problematic, because geese do not have kneecaps.

Pity that the Katrina victims didn't take PenMar up on its offer of housing. A ready made food supply could have been part of the deal.

Of course you can't destroy them, so Rook said the best techniques will be employed "short of a shotgun."

It's always curious to me what is and isn't acceptable for society to kill. You can kill a deer or a bear, but not a goose or a crow. Who decided that? So we wind up doing crazy things like spraying the downtown with the scent of grapes. So now we don't have any crows, but we are being overrun by the French.

Of course all it would take is one little case of bird flu to change the minds of a prone-to-panic public. The geese better watch themselves. If one of them sneezes they may be in for a mass slaughter.

But at this point in time we remain goose-friendly, so this opens the door for Dan Laxton, whom I know and admire from his rafting days on the Shenandoah, and his "Gone in a Zip" goose solution business to come in and do the job. Dan didn't ask me for help with the name — I might have gone with "Goose Vamoose Inc." I checked, and goosevamoose.com is still an available domain name, so he'd have first-mover status.

Zip is a border collie, and is part of what appears to be a 73-step goose eradication program that vaguely resembles the old game of "Mousetrap," although not as straightforward. Other "tools of the trade" include hip waders, a kayak and a remote-control boat. All that's missing is a trapeze. You see those items grouped together and you don't know eat a bird patrol or the setting of a porn shoot.

"Uh-oh, here comes naughty Gretchen in her remote-controlled boat..."

Dan says the methods employed amount to "humane goose harassment." You just keep after them and keep after them with all the weapons at your disposal until they get bothered and leave. It's a shame we didn't know about this when they were having trouble with loiterers in front of the Washington County Circuit Courthouse. That would have been so much more amusing than just removing the benches.

And if I am allowed to take my fantasies that far in our little goosecapade, I would like to go one step further and suggest that the border collie "chasers" be replaced with members of the PenMar board of directors.

Or if bothering them to death is the goal, wouldn't it be easier to just show up on their doorstep and hand out religious tracts? Of course It's been years since I've seen any of those guys, particularly at the airports. Leave it to Homeland Security to make me nostalgic for the Krishas.

Speaking of flying, what ever happened to the days when the geese used to migrate? Used to be, you would only see geese in those big V's up about 2,000 feet on their way south. Now, it's like they get to Hagerstown and say, screw it, this is far enough.

I didn't realize instinct could be deprogrammed that easily. Toss them a little white bread at City Park, and all of sudden 10 million years of evolution goes right down the flume.

Seems that we could use that to our advantage in the spots where the geese population has taken over. Instead of corn, we could throw them morning-after pills. If I'm a goose, tell me that isn't better than being chased by a remote controlled boat.

Manly Men Hunters Slow to Draw as Girl, 8, Gets Bear

Horrible, horrible news on the battle-of-the-sexes front. Horrible if you're a guy, that is. Maryland's second annual bear hunt commenced this week, and the first person to bag a Yogi was not some great and grizzled warrior of the woods.

It was not a Daniel Boone, a Roosevelt rough rider or an "Old Mountain" Phelps. No, the first person to kill themselves a b'ar was an 8-year-old kid.

An 8-year-old she kid.

Somewhere, Davy Crockett is spinning in his coonskin cap.

Sierra Stiles, a third-grader from Western Maryland, shouldered a .243 rifle and killed a 211-pound male bear, the first of 13 to be taken on the initial day of the hunt.

How did this happen? What, a teddy bear not good enough for her? There's a photo of Sierra, a cute blond kid, sitting on the bed of a pickup, the burly beast sprawled out behind her.

First of all, if I'm this bear's family, I'm rounding up every last one of these photos I can find and burning them. Talk about an indignity. There's the man of the house, the mighty and fearsome grubwinner, flat on his back with his eyes X-ed out, and a grinning, apple-cheeked third-grader resting her elbow on his neck.

This has to be the Homer Simpson of bears. "Oh look, it's a nice little girlie sitting in the middle of the for ... d'oh!"

Second, I would have liked to have had a word with this animal prior to Goldilocks' revenge. I mean, come on, guy! You can't go out an let yourself get undressed by a giggling, Pixie Stix- eating, doll house tender. At least make an effort. She's the beauty, you're the beast, would it have killed you to rise up on your hind legs and disgorged a mighty, terrorizing roar? Come to think of it, it might have. Well, at least feel free to duck.

And third, I have a word for all you big, husky, full-grown male hunters. Two words, actually:

For shame. For shame, for shame, for shame. Do you realize how few areas of male domination we have left? There's that Japanese dude who can eat more hot dogs than anyone else — except, ironically enough, for a bear, thank you very much Fox television for that indispensable bit of information. And I think we still put in a pretty good show every year in the remote control Olympics, but outside of that, women are passing us in every area with alarming speed.

I would have thought hunting was relatively sacred ground, if nothing else than for the fact that a sizable percentage of women think it's disgusting. You know how it is, guy goes out big game hunting and comes home and sticks the heads in the freezer while he's on the taxidermist's waiting list. Then every time she goes hunting up a pound of ground chuck she's got an elk staring her in the chops. They don't like that, for some reason.

But even this is changing. In fact, two of the first three bears taken in Monday's hunt were killed by women, and another bear was killed by a 9-year-old girl from Garrett County.

Looks as if the women have a better farm team, probably because all the boys are home playing video war games. "Anywhere you go for hunting these days, you see a lot more women," Tera Roach, a 23-year-old receptionist from Reisterstown who shot a 147-pound bear in Garrett County, told The Baltimore Sun.

Thanks a lot, chickie poos. Couldn't let us have just this one last bastion of male retreat, could you? First VMI, then poker, now bear hunting. Whatever happened to the good old days when the only thing you did with powder was put it on your nose?

And for the most part, we men have gone without a fight. Oh sure, there were a few bumper stickers that said, "Virginia Military Institute will start accepting women when the University of Virginia starts accepting men," but that was about it.

It's unfair, because with the advent of hunter safety tests, they can even trump us with intellect. Young Sierra scored a 98 on her safety test. This explains why there weren't more boys in the hunt.

Test: "If you see movement in the forest, shoot before you know what it is so it doesn't get away."

Boy: "What do you mean, 'false'?"

When I was a kid, I remember a classmate on the first day of deer season who hit upon the brilliant idea of draping a deer hide over his shoulders and tying antlers to his head so the deer would think he was one of them. Now they make you wear so much orange, the woods look as if they are full of construction zone flagmen.

When a man's native genius is stunted so, is it any wonder we're falling further and further behind?

They Will Not Let Me Rest

For the past three years I have traditionally used the first day of deer season to recount the series of bizarre deer hunting stories that have taken place during the previous 12 months.

There was once the guy in West Virginia who shot himself while cleaning his rifle. Not once, not twice, but three times.

There was the man in St. Louisville, Ohio, who stabbed himself when he was cleaning a deer because the deer contorted and drove the knife into his (the hunter's) right leg. His comment to police was that he "thought the deer was deader than it was."

But this year had been relatively calm, deerly speaking, and I was hoping to be able to use this space for an educated essay on trade barriers or something.

But no. With the coffee this morning came the report of a frantic buck that burst through the IRS office in nearby Martinsburg, W.Va., and thoroughly trashed the place.

First, let me make it clear from the beginning: This deer was not on my payroll.

Although I do believe it was more than a coincidence that the animal picked a tax office to destroy. The IRS probably notified him that he could no longer claim an 80 percent deduction on salt licks and entertainment during business trips and he just snapped. Or maybe he thought IRS stood for International Rutting Service.

Police said the deer was a trophy-size buck. "Trophy size, does that mean it was about this high?" asked a colleague, holding his hands apart about the length of a standard bowling trophy. My colleague doesn't hunt much.

Actually, this was the second wacky deer story of the year. The first came from my parents who let a friend bow hunt on their property a couple weeks back.

The man shot a deer, which bounded off a piece before it dropped. After a search, they discovered not one, but two dead deer. The arrow had traveled through one and into a second that had apparently been directly behind it.

This is why I always say it is never good to stand too close to your friends.

Police finally had to shoot the Martinsburg IRS deer (I don't know whether they used a 30-30 or a 10-40. Both are just as deadly in the long run). They said it was probably startled because of activity in the woods on the eve of deer season.

Personally though, I believe the deer was still celebrating over West Virginia's 17-14 college football victory over Miami.

This was perhaps the single best win I can remember in West Virginia football history, with the exception, of course, of any win over Pitt.

It may have been the most exciting West Virginia game I've seen since the 1984 game against Boston College, when BC was No. 4 in the country and led by Heisman candidate Doug Flutie. West Virginia won that one 21-20 after trailing 20-6 at the half.

I was on the sidelines during the game because I had, uh, procured a photo pass. Technically, people with photo passes are supposed to be shooting photos of the game and I technically passed as a photographer because I borrowed a friend's camera. I was not, however, able to fulfill the traditional role of the photojournalist in that I was unschooled in some of the finer points of sports photography, such as how to turn on the light meter.

But I had fun watching the game up close through the 500 millimeter lens. Until Flutie completed a pass to a receiver who was leaping out of control and about to smash directly into me.

With panther-like instincts I dove screaming out of the receiver's way.

What I should have realized at the time, but didn't, was that because I was watching the action through a powerful telephoto lens the receiver was still about 30 yards upfield — nowhere near me.

I looked up to see the row of professional photographers staring at me with puzzled expressions as I lay sprawled on the ground, encircled by scattered lenses and rolls of film.

It was at that point that I decided to watch the remainder of the game from the Boston College side of the field.

Cutting Down on Deer Carnage

If you're looking for a good legislative agenda to get behind as the Maryland General Assembly fires into action this week, may I suggest you need look no further that the goals set forward by Del. Joe Bartlett, R-Frederick/Washington.

In a legislative preview in a regional publication, one State House correspondent wrote that Bartlett "has plans to restore respect to the teaching profession and reduce the number of deer killed on the state's roads."

I couldn't agree more on these priorities. Although I know how the legislature works, and with our luck they'll end up restoring respect to deer and passing a law to keep teachers from jumping out in front of cars.

Now that I think about it though, respect for teachers is overrated. If you give them respect, then they'll want decent pay and then they'll want parents to be responsible and then they'll want administrators to leave them the heck alone so they can just teach already — there will be no end to it. If I'm passing the laws I'm willing to legislate them some, "go as far as "grudging admiration," but out-and-out respect just opens up too many cans of worms.

But the deer issue, there's one I can fully endorse because I'm guessing Joe Bartlett has noticed the same thing I have, which is that the interstates anymore are lined with more carcasses than a Hormel meat packing plant.

The corpses are so thick that on Halloween I was considering charging the deer admission to walk up and down I-70 as part of a cervine spine-chilling haunted house tour.

Even so, it's not as bad as Pennsylvania, where if I were PennDOT I'd simply strap a sausage grinder onto a snowplow and turn a profit. Pappa PenDOT's Pure Potted Porklike Patty Product. Now with 50 percent fewer antlers. Umm-mm.

Bartlett's plan doesn't involve a sausage grinder, but it would require cars licensed in Maryland to be equipped with those tiny, silent whistles you always see advertised in the Spencer Gifts catalog right next to the novelty beer-barrel corn holders and ice cube trays shaped like Richard Nixon.

The whistles, which can only be heard by deer and state lawmakers, are wind-activated and theoretically emit a high-pitched noise that sends deer scurrying in the other direction when your car comes within a half-mile or so.

A mandatory deer whistle program shouldn't cost the state too much money to set up, since they could just piggyback the bureaucracy on the Vehicle Emission Inspection Program (VEIP).

Every other year you would get your Deer Inspection Program (DeIP) notification along with your Vehicle Emission Inspection Program notification and you would take your car into the state testing garage.

First they would put your car on a treadmill to check the exhaust, then they would put it in a wind tunnel to check the silent whistles. The state would have a deer standing in a nearby pen, and if he clamps his hooves over his ears and screams "Noooo!!" then you pass.

And best of all, the state MVA would be able to charge you $35 for the service of testing your deer whistles, making it a win-win for both the deer and the state treasury.

For the Maryland motorist, it's a small price to pay to know there won't be a deer lurking behind every tree just waiting for the chance to accordion your sheet metal.

And who knows, this could be the beginning of many great state-critter programs. I don't want to say this too loud in case Joe Bartlett may be listening, but I have noticed a lot of flattened groundhogs by the side of the road lately.

The Groundhogs Must Die

License to kill gophers by the government of the United Nations. Man, free to kill gophers at will. To kill, you must know your enemy, and in this case my enemy is a varmint. And a varmint will never quit — ever. They're like the Viet Cong — Varmint Cong. So you have to lie back on superior intelligence and superior firepower.

And that's all she wrote. — Carl Spackler in Caddyshack

The woodchuck awoke Sunday morning to discover the rules had changed. Oh, he'd been having a pretty free time of it. Living high on the groundhog you reason.

I had noticed he'd eaten the cabbages down to the ground, but I didn't say anything. Then he stripped the broccoli down to a single stem, making it look as if I'd planted a long row of drumsticks. I didn't say anything.

Next he had a go at the beets. The only edible part of a beet, in my view, is the top, and on this issue the groundhog and I must have similar opinions, because that's the part he got. But even then I didn't say anything.

It was interesting in a way. He would scurry from his hole past the beans, past the tomatoes, past the onions, past the squash and past the zinnias to get to the broccoli/cabbage quadrant.

I thought that showed a lot of self-restraint for a rodent. You have to admire a groundhog who knows what he likes.

But then he made a key error; he scarfed down the cantaloupes. That made it personal.

I solicited and received all sorts of advice, from mothballs to peanut-butter baited traps to antifreeze-soaked apples.

Let it never be said that the word "overkill" is part of my vocabulary, because after hearing all these opinions I selected all of the above.

It would be a sort of the carpet-bomb approach to woodchucks. I walked up to the cashier with eggs, Dr. Pepper, antifreeze, peanut butter, Zip-Loc bags, mothballs, rubber bands, apples, a squirt-bottle and cayenne powder and she gives me one of those looks that says "what you do at home at night is your own business mister, just leave me out of it" and then I packed it all into Old Copper and set out for the blueberry ranch.

Morally, I was aided in my plan in that women don't find groundhogs cute. Squirrels? "You can't hurt a squirrel, they're so cute." Rabbits? "You can't hurt a bunny, they're so cute." Deer? "You can't hurt a deer, they're so cute." Groundhogs? "Eh, do what you have to."

It's the four and 20 blackbirds paradigm. Had they been indigo buntings, I guarantee they never would have been subjected to the indignities of pastry filling.

So Saturday night I mobilized. I affixed the vegetable garden with more booby traps than the 1968 Mekong Delta. If that critter had hit the trip-wire just right he'd have been hurled to Winchester.

But based on some forensic crime scene recreation on my part the next day, he never made it past the apple slices. I confess to chickening out with the antifreeze. I went with mouthwash. I didn't want to kill him, just get him real sick.

People familiar with my cooking suggested I soak the apples in some of my homemade vichyssoise, and for a moment I did consider windshield washing fluid. From what I can gather it's a little poisonous, but if diluted it would do no more harm than a bad stomachache. The antifreeze jug had a skull and bones on the label; the washer fluid had a skull and bones, but there was also a little happy face next to the antidote.

Anyway, I don't know what apple and mouthwash tastes like, but based on pawprints in the garden it must be pretty awful, because that groundhog left the county in three jumps exactly.

Now I can't wait until he comes back. If he liked the mouthwash, he's going to love the moth balls soaked in Dr. Pepper.

Got a Deer in the Trunk of My Light Blue Mercedes

Blame it on Lyle Lovett. I don't get to hear too much country music, but Lyle shifts from blues up to jazz down to country smoother than a Ferrari gearbox, so sometimes before I know it he's off on something like "I Married Her Because She Looks Like You."

Now if you're like me, and I assume that you are, there is something about listening to country that makes you want to write country music.

It's like watching a field goal kicker. You hear the line "my wife just ran away with my best friend and I miss him" and think "I could do that." All you need is some inspiration.

Flash back to last Tuesday when my colleague (and designated eye witness, should anyone doubt my story) Laura Ernde and I were returning from a withering day of lawmaker interviews in Annapolis. Well, she was interviewing. But I superintended.

So you can imagine, tired as I was, I didn't exactly trust my eyes when I saw a couple deer stuffed into the trunk of a car on I-97 just outside of Baltimore.

Now keep in mind I live in Hagerstown. I am used to seeing deer carci in the beds of pickups, strapped to roofs and yes, on rare occasion, sticking out of a trunk. And Laura lives in Pennsylvania where people do not drive cars so much as they drive deer snowplows.

But what truly startled us was the type of car involved — a blue, late model, top-of-the-line Mercedes Benz.

Had the Lord actually bought Janis Joplin a Mercedes Benz, she might have been the type to drive around with gutted wildlife in the trunk. But a normal person?

I know some doctors who like to hunt, but the deer are eminently safe when they are in the woods so long as they stand still, although sometimes they get moving around and a stray slug hits them by accident.

And I know some MBAs who like to shoot, but they limit their lead output to flying clay disks that give you the satisfying sense of destruction without all that blood.

But what if there were one broker out there who one day just snapped. Got fed up with daily market palpitations, bought a 30-30 and didn't even bother stopping off to get a sport utility vehicle — just headed straight for the woods.

And what if he got lucky and mowed down a couple whitetail? It could happen. And if id did, he might just find himself singing something like this:

Oh I'm an investment banker, in the Wall Street Journal loop.
Built a house of cards and money, sail a custom Hinkley sloop.
I hedge junk bond derivatives and buy options on soy and cotton.
The pressure kills I got a stack of bills,
And the future sure looks rotten.

The market it's up on a ledge and I'll be there shortly now.
Or in a padded room at Betty Ford's right next to Steve Howe.
I got to blow this stress off, get me a gun and hurry.
Ditch these rich neighborhoods and head for the woods,
So's I can blow up something furry.

Now I'm cruising the Beltway in lane number three
peoples turning their heads theys all smiling at me
I'll earn the respect of my boss score points with the ladies
With two deer in the trunk of my light blue Mercedes.
Got two deer in the trunk, going out on the town.
Don't care if the blood turns the carpet dark brown.
Their rumps are bobbin up and down on the fender,
It may dent the metal but it'll make the chops tender

The cellular phone goes in the trash as I head for my garage.
I've traded in my Armani suit for blaze orange camouflage.
Sometimes you need a life change to get that frustration out.
Need to perk up my luck got to bag me a buck,
That will make me a man, no doubt.
(Repeat chorus.)

All right. it's not Lyle Lovett, but what do you want for 50 cents?

Onix Dares to Follow in Bucky's Prized Footsteps

No, no, please, a thousand times no. Not another critter on the lam story.

Didn't we learn our lesson with Bucky the Deer? Now we have Onix the Raccoon. Pretty soon we will have news choppers hovering overhead and graphics and dotted lines with the subhead "Raccoon's Path."

I can't take it.

Department of Natural Resources spokeswoman Heather Lynch has to be wondering why she didn't pick a career as a systems analyst or something. Here she is again, explaining to the public that wild animals can't be pets.

Well, they can be pets, but Maryland law says they can't, so that settles things.

Last we heard from Heather, she was wearily explaining that you can't have a deer in your foyer (unless it's stuffed) and expect the DNR to sit idly by and do nothing about it. Bucky, you remember, was taken in by a family who said they saved it from Most Favored Roadkill status as it stumbled around Eastern Boulevard.

The family wanted to save it, but the DNR wanted to kill it so it could be tested for something akin to Bubonic Deer Plague. Well, that led to a volcanic eruption of public angst, and negotiations that, for intensity, made the Iranian hostage crisis look like traffic court. Bucky was eventually, and surreptitiously, set free in the wild, where he was immediately eaten by wolves.

Now comes Onix the Raccoon, the 13-year pet of a Keedysville couple that wandered off from a cage and was picked up by the Humane Society (the raccoon, not the couple).

So, as they say in the horror flick business, it's all happening again.

Some things Onix has going for it, some things it doesn't. On the negative side of the ledger is the name "Onix." It's an OK name, but frankly, it is not a cute name. "Bucky" was a cute and playful name. "Onix" doesn't sound like anything you would want to cuddle. It's just a little too abstract and scientific. If the family could travel 13 years back in time, they might do well to choose a name like "Spunky" or "Binky" or "Pamela Anderson."

On the plus side, a raccoon is a moderately cute animal. Not as sympathetically cute as a fawn, perhaps, but more so than a muskrat. They get cute points for washing their food, but lose some of these for their regrettable habit of rummaging through trash bins.

So now Onix, if that is his real name, is a political prisoner of the Humane Society. Since you can't debrief a raccoon, they can't unlearn him of his domestic ways and set him loose in the wild. And without a permit, a family cannot keep a wild animal as a pet.

But Onix's owner, C.J. Giffin, put up a good point. If the Maryland Department of Natural Resources had been around and wielding authority in the days of the Pharaohs, there would be no such thing today as a domesticated dog or cat.

But the DNR isn't about to be drawn into the argument of who should have domesticated whom, or whether the whole situation might have been different if Ramses II snuggled up next to a Procyn Lotor instead of a Felinus Whateverus.

So if the poor beast can't be relocated to some kind of educational petting zoo, it's going to have to be — how to put this delicately so as not to upset the children — well, let's just say that Davy Crockett is going to wake up with one cap too many.

Fortunately, Giffin isn't the only one who is Hooked on Onix. Yes, the raccoon has an attorney. Jerome "Ranger Rick" Joyce said last week he will represent the raccoon for free because, "as a child I always wanted a pet raccoon."

Well, yes, lots of kids have wanted a pet raccoon. But, to be brutally honest, most of them got over it by age 12. No, I don't mean that — it's just that I'm bitter that a raccoon gets a lawyer for free, while I can't find one that will represent me for any price.

Joyce points out that the Giffin-raccoon relationship has lasted longer than most marriages — which is true, but then again, when was the last time you saw a raccoon buy his wife a vacuum cleaner for her birthday? And please, they only live to be about 16, anyway. (Raccoons also have a top speed of 15 mph — who says I don't do research?) So Onix is like on Social Raccoon Security.

I hope we can "bend the rules" a bit and "look the other way" so we can "gloss over" this unpleasantness and move on to other clichés, such as, all's well that ends pelt, I mean welt, I mean well.

To Protect the Presidential Retreat, the Buck Stops Here

Any source that is a threat to presidents and ground-nesting birds must be dealt with severely.

In these stressful times, National Park Service rangers at Catoctin Mountain Park are understandably concerned about the safety of the presidential retreat known as Camp David.

Camp David, they say, is under a real and present threat. It is a threat so credible that they plan to take immediate action — or as immediate as government action ever gets, which is to say about two or three years down the road.

And what desperate group is behind this assault on one of our national icons? Al-Qaida? Abu Nidal? Al-Jihad? Hamas? Hizballah? The Liberation Tigers of Tamil Eelam? No, although that last one's close.

It's the deer.

Rangers say Catoctin Mountain has become the virtual Calcutta of deer population. There are so many that every scrap of vegetation below the 6-foot level has been eaten, and that lack of undergrowth "threatens the privacy of Camp David," according to a story from the Associated Press.

We're still waiting for some fringe deer faction such as the Talibuck to claim responsibility for this defoliation, but in the meantime rangers are mulling the options for what will be known as Operation Indeering Freedom.

This is important, because along with destroying Camp David secrecy, the deer are also destroying a healthy ecology, says park Resource Manager James Voigt.

"If you're a ground-nesting bird that needs that underbrush, it's not real good," Voigt said.

So this situation must be rectified, and the park is considering ways to reduce the deer population.

Unfortunately it has ruled out the introduction of natural, ravenous predators such as mountain lions or Rosie O'Donnell. This would endanger local livestock, which is too bad because they might also cut down on the burgeoning number of tourists from D.C. who clog up the trails and treat Catoctin like it's Mt. Everest with their Gore-Tex and their backpacks and their approach shoes and their doggie saddlebags and their stinking baby packs and ... what? oh, sorry.

The other option I like is simply to shoot them. People say that's my solution to everything, but even as generally pro-critter as I am, it seems far preferable to me to establish a controlled hunt than to allow the deer population to expand to the point deer begin to starve to death.

The Humane Society doesn't think so, and rangers fear the agency would bring a delaying lawsuit against the park. Still, it may be their only choice since a third option, deer birth control, may not work well on free-ranging herds. Although, rangers swear birth control injections and contraceptives work on more controlled deer populations.

Well. The thought of a Deer Intrauterine (DIU) application is enough to give one pause. Or hooves, as the case may be. I don't know how else you would do it, however, unless we paper the woods with those "Virgin is not a bad word" billboards.

It's a critical point, in keeping with a story by reporter Kim Yakowski that a reader wanted to be sure I saw — headlined "Deer mating dangerous for drivers." According to the article, this is the time of year when deer lose track of all else (including traffic) in pursuit of a mate. Since there is no written warning on automobile glass such as "Objects in mirror may be more sex-crazed than they appear," drivers are warned to be alert on their own.

Your chances of hitting a deer or Bill Clinton exponentially increase each fall because "a buck will mate with as many females as he can find," said state deer expert Doug Hotton.

Typical, government-sponsored male-bashing, I say. If you think about it though, this information may offer a solution for the predicament up at Camp Donner. These single-minded bucks need a diversion. Park rangers might be able to distract them with the introduction not of mountain lions, but of beer and football games.

Goats are the Comedians of the Barnyard

Whenever I visit Ag Expo, I wind up spending most of my time with the goats. Don't try to read anything into that.

The fact is, I want one. No, two. Or more. So Sunday was sort of like a shopping trip, as we strolled past pens of Alpines, LaManchas, Boers, Nubians and one Toggenburg.

The thing is, if goats were people, they would be newspaper columnists.

They think everything is funny, take nothing seriously and are prototypical wise guys. They are good at extracting themselves from tight spaces. It's said that if a fence can't hold water, it can't hold a goat.

I had three Toggenburgs when I was 14, which basically was a 4-H project gone horribly wrong. If they weren't on the roof of their house, they were on the car, or stripping leaves off of an azalea.

Deer eat your prize shrubs because they're hungry. Goats eat your prize shrubs because it makes for a great joke.

I raised a beautiful pasture of red clover and timothy, turned the goat, Crystal, out in the middle of it. She gave it a disdainful survey, then calmly proceeded to the center of the patch where one lone milkweed poked its head up above the grass. She bit it off, and then chewed on it for about 10 minutes, staring icily at me the whole while.

She was not an animal to be told what to do.

Effectively, goats are dogs that you don't have to walk. Matter of fact, being led around is not their strength — something those who were showing their goats at the fair would probably agree with.

The dairy goats will follow you around peacefully enough, but the meat goats, not so much.

Probably this is because the dairy goats know that if they follow you they will get food; the meat goats know if they follow you they will become food.

We were keenly attentive to the judge's criticisms in the ring, as he commented on each entry, explaining what made the animal worthy or not.

Beth decided that goats ought to be the heroes of women everywhere — since desirability was associated with a thick midsection and a round bottom. If men judged women the same way, the nation's dating scene would be turned on its head.

At this point, we haven't decided whether we're opting for dairy goats or meat goats. We have two already — Pete and Eddie — but they are shaggy, long-horned and strictly ornamental. If they were not goats they would be in the Mafia. Pete, especially.

Their only other function is for amusement and as a rather guilt-free way of disposing of surplus zucchini. Until they figured out that we WANTED them to eat the surplus zucchini, at which point they lost their taste for the produce.

Dairy goats are elegant, friendly and sassy. But you have to milk them. Twice a day. Every day. Ten months out of the year.

For a male, this takes the commitment issue with females to a whole new level. This would be like having a wife who — oh, never mind.

For obvious reasons, people don't get as attached to meat goats, so they tend to be wilder and more aloof. You don't want a critter who is first in your heart to wind up first in the stew.

Yet I'm told that worldwide, goats account for something like 70 percent of red meat consumption. But this is not the rest of the world. Our meat selection is inversely proportional to the degree of animal cuteness — which, frankly, is a baby goat's chief commodity.

Pigs are born cute and grow up to be slovenly. No problem there. Chickens evolved from dinosaurs and look it. Cows — I don't know, it's hard to be cute and weigh 1,500 pounds. (By the way, mad props for the kids at the expo who named their cattle after diesel engines: "Powerstroke," "Cummins," "Duramax." I like that.)

Because of the low maintenance angle however, I'm currently leaning toward the nondairy side of the equation. It's not as if my standing with PETA could get any worse.

And when we sell the kids, I will just assume they are all going to good homes. I will thank the abattoir not to tell me any different.

Meat Eaters Among Us

Earlier this month, a representative from People for the Ethical Treatment of Animals snuck into a lecture hall and clowned Secretary of Agriculture Dan Glickman with a tofu cream pie.

Lucky for PETA, I'm not secretary of agriculture, for I guarantee you at the next PETA convention there would be some hemp-attired, sunscreen wearing, Ralph Nader-voting committee chairperson wearing a steak and kidney cream pie.

Sorry, but I'm just an Old Testament kind of guy. I believe in a tooth for a tooth and a pie for a pie.

Besides, I have to question PETA's tactics. It's been scientifically demonstrated that greater health risks accompany meat consumption as opposed to plates of fruit, vegetables and grains. So why would PETA want people with a spite against animals to switch over to a life-prolonging diet?

Seems they'd want us to "eat meat and die," so to speak.

And I have one other quandary I'd like to put to the wild kingdom and its protectors. I like vegetables. I love vegetables, in fact. And I would like to eat more of them — but the animals won't let me. As I write this, I am virtually certain there is a tag team of groundhogs and deer leveling my broccoli to the length of a putting green.

Yet so far as I know, there is no "human rights" group forming among members of the animal world with my interests at heart. If we adopt PETA's policy we will all sit by and quietly starve as the animal hoards decimate our soybeans.

Anyway, I heard a National Public Radio report shortly after the pieing incident where some stuffy old fellow was grumbling that pulling stunts such as hurling pastry at bureaucrats cheapened serious efforts to protect animals and promote healthier eating habits.

Oh, please. Look, for the sake of argument, say that you are trying to make a point to the American public. Do you:

A.) Call a press conference and, flanked by a team of scientists, present tables and charts depicting global nutritional trends and juxtapose them against projections assuming a greater soy-based consumption model.

B.) Throw a pie in someone's face.

I don't know that PETA's action proves that we should eat more vegetable protein, but the one thing it does prove conclusively is that we are a nation of idiots.

PETA knows we don't have a prayer of noodling through a comprehensive agriculture policy. It realizes that about all our neurological circuitry groomed and honed by a billion years of evolution has the capability of achieving is nudging the person next to us on the couch and saying "Look, Klem. Ha-ha. A pie."

Speaking of evolution, I'd be curious to know what PETA's thoughts are about the news last week that our Neanderthal ancestors ate a diet that consisted almost exclusively of meat. Wouldn't it be a great stunt of they could invent a time machine and travel back to the stone age to throw a pie in the face of a guy named Oog?

Maybe a little education would have helped. Perhaps the Neanderthals had all been brainwashed by catchy slogans from the Prehistoric Meat Council, like:

"Tyranospecterpherasaurous — The other white meat." Or, "Mastodon: It's what's for dinner."

But at least they only ate free-range mammoths. And I guess PETA has always considered us modern-day meat eaters to be Neanderthals, so maybe it all fits.

Which reminds me, after writing this I better go Tofuguard my coat.

Watching Opie Learn Life's Lessons is Fun Homework

His breed is a Bouvier des Flandres.

If you ask me, that's a pretty pretentious title for a dog. So to take him down a peg, we named him "Opie."

Grace and agility are never strengths in a puppy, but this one took a lack of coordination to new levels. As a matter of fact, he fell over more often than a two-legged bar stool — so much so that for a time we seriously considered naming him "Thud."

Opie is a big black mop of a dog, and although he will top out at close to 100 pounds, at the moment the Bouvier rather resembles a 35-pound bear cub — or a black sheepdog, but with more hair.

You know he must have eyes in there somewhere, but you can't much see them. When he looks at you, it's kind of like being stared at by a boxwood.

I'd never been around a puppy full time before. And while I'm still no expert, I have learned some things, whether I wanted to or not.

For example, I believe that puppies have not one, but two tiny little brains. One brain controls the front legs, while the other lords over the aft.

And the two brains never communicate.

He'll be lumbering along in pursuit of something known only to him, when Brain 1 will instruct the front legs to slam on the brakes. Brain 1, however, does not bother to convey this message to Brain 2, so consequently, while the front legs are slowing down, the rear legs continue to accelerate.

The result is almost unwatchable.

If you wish to recreate what happens in the comfort of your own neighborhood, take your bike to the nearest steep hill, get up a ton of speed and then slam on the front brakes only.

After about the fifth somersault, Opie's pinwheeling momentum will slow to a stop, just as the hindquarters are reaching an apex above the forequarters. This upside-down pillar of dog will hold that pose for a half second, before the whole furry black mass collapses on itself in a pile of doggie rubble featuring bones bending in ways that they are not intended to bend.

But does he care? No, because he is a puppy, and puppies do not care about anything. Everything is fun. Falling down the stairs is a carnival, running full-speed into a wall is a Mediterranean cruise. You can't punish the animal, because he takes even the harshest word as encouragement and applause. His only regret about getting swatted by cat claws is that it doesn't happen more often.

Beth's cat, a small but intense Siamese named Juliet, finally gave up. Not that she didn't try. Lord knows she tried.

But a feline only has so many claws and so much energy. After raking her barbed paws across Opie's dome for the umpteenth time — only to see her victim bounce up and down with the joy that comes from being noticed — Juliet washed her hands of the whole project and developed the strategy of hanging out in a nearby tree where she could view the carnage from above.

With the cat out of the picture, Opie went to work on Hannah, an English bulldog with the dignity of an English butler and the worries of a Jewish grandmother.

Mixing Opie and Hannah was like mixing Kid Rock with George Will.

But it couldn't be helped. After three weeks, Hannah condescended to play with Opie. Well, maybe it was play, maybe it was attempted murder, it was hard to tell.

It all reached a boiling point one afternoon when the bulldog — 44 pounds of fur and phlegm — raised herself off of her prone position on the sidewalk, leaving a puddle of drool, as she always does. She waddled stoically into the yard to perform that most sacred of dog rituals.

Hannah primly fluffed herself up and after some research, found just the right spot in the lawn next to the flower bed. She squatted and had just slowly closed her eyes to commence her peaceful, urinary liturgy when, out of nowhere, she was broadsided by a flying Bouvier.

The resulting tornadic tumbleweed of grass, dust, gaillardia, dog and yellow spray would have made the Super Bowl halftime show look like poetry reading.

There was a coolness between Hannah and Opie after that stunt, so recently Opie has been eying the goats as potential playmates.

These goats don't do much to earn their keep, other than to look picturesque. They are shaggy, long-horned, purely ornamental, just-add-Heidi goats. But they do love to butt, with a vengeance. And they love nothing more than a good prank.

As Opie gets braver and wanders ever closer to their pasture, I can't help but think that this ought to be good.

Glorified Billy Goats Valued for Cuteness

Looking back on it, I'm not entirely sure how we wound up with four alpacas. It was almost as if we woke up one morning and they were there. True, we had been "testing the waters" for some time, visiting local alpaca ranches and signing up for alpaca newsletters.

Near as I can tell, alpacas —which resemble scaled-down, shaggy, humpless camels —have four solid attributes in their favor:

1. They are very cute.
2. They don't eat much.
3. They are very cute.
4. In many circles, they are seen as very cute.

They are also Very Valuable, for reasons I haven't quite gotten to the bottom of. Let me qualify that. They are Very Valuable if they are capable of breeding; if they are incapable of breeding, not so much. In that way, they are sort of like 1980s-era welfare programs.

Being a journalist, it is unlikely that I will be laying out $20,000 on a female alpaca or $150,000 for a champion herd sire. Our new silver alpaca named Sterling would have been one of the latter, except that — and I describe this at the risk of agitating Del. LeRoy Myers — one of his testicles did not pop into place, so instead of selling for $150,000, he sold for $500.

This should be a sober lesson for males of every species. Without our reproductive proclivities, we would be viewed as so much useless protoplasm, barely worth cost of the hay it takes to keep us alive.

So with one exception, ours are pretty much pets — placeholder text, so to speak, to see if this is an enterprise we want to get into on a greater scale. And of course, when I say "we" I mean "Beth." Although I confess, they are tough critters not to get attached to with a quickness.

The exception that I mentioned is a high-quality herd sire named Copperfield that we bought from a farm in Kentucky for the standard $500 pet cost because the ranch had too many males — sort of the opposite problem of what they have in China, I take it.

But now it seems there was some kind of internal "misunderstanding" and he shouldn't have been let go at this price. So while they work it out — and being good people, I'm sure they will — the farm is temporarily withholding his paperwork, which, apparently, is more valuable than the animal itself.

It's much ado about a glorified billy goat, in my opinion, and we're pretty pleased with Copper, whether he comes with his own personal Magna Carta or not.

And the tall, elegant, coal-black Copperfield certainly doesn't care. He immediately made himself comfortable with his new, self-appointed role as the barnyard pope, lording over the donkeys, goats and dogs with a calm, regal benevolence that comes with the knowledge that everything on the 15 acres revolves around him.

The bouvier des Flandres named Opie had kind of served in this role up until last week — with the exception of the "calm, regal benevolence" part. Opie ruled with a scepter of enthusiasm and a crown of frenzy.

Using these tools, the only ones he knows, he immediately tried to bring Copper, Sterling and the other two members of the nativity scene under his paw with the usual sprints, dives, leaps and ostentatious head tossing.

He might have saved himself the swashbuckling, because King Copper, for one, clearly was not impressed.

Opie was used to large farm animals bolting away in submission, but what had worked in the past failed in the present. Copperfield merely strolled over to Opie with all the urgency of a highway worker and lowered his ample neck toward the dog with a bemused, "what have we hereness" that knocked Opie completely off stride.

Poor dog. He hasn't quite been the same since. He's taken to long, quiet bouts of meditation and introspection until he can figure out what this new turn of events means. When he finds out, I hope he lets me know.

A Hay Bale a Day Keeps the Animals at Bay...and Fed

I'm a bit concerned with the price of gas, yes. But I never imagined I would spend more time fretting over the price of hay.

It's not as if we're real farmers; it's just that our pets are bigger than most people's. Donkeys, horses, alpacas, goats — if we had lived in biblical times, we could have provided Noah with a serious shortcut when he was rounding up inventory.

So, needless to say, the pet food doesn't come from a can, it comes from a bale. And as comforting as the purr of a kitty can be, it is equaled by the sound of the big guys tranquilly munching hay on a still, frosty morning.

Twice a day, Beth and I make the rounds with a wheelbarrow full of the fragrant dried plant life, visiting the animals in order of their nagging. The donkeys are by far the worst. They don't really "hee-haw" in the strict sense of the word, but they belch out a rather horrifying vocal atrocity that sounds as if they are being gutted and fileted by a butcher who hasn't sharpened his knife for a couple of months.

By contrast, the four alpacas simply hum in a rather whimsical fashion. We read that you can feed 60 alpacas on a bale of hay a day, and maybe you can if the bale is the size of a refrigerator.

All told, we are going through some serious forage. This might not be much of an issue in normal years, but with the drought last summer, farmers were lucky to get one cutting instead of three. So hay this winter is scarce and expensive, making me feel for the people who depend on the commodity for their livelihoods. Prices are going north of $5 a bale, or double that of normal years.

Frankly, I think the Mail Call contributors are missing out on a serious issue here.

"Hi Mail Call, can anyone tell me why hay is 50 cents more a bale in Washington County than it is right across the line in ..."

I saw hay advertised for $2.75 a bale in New York this summer, and if I'd thought about it, I would have rented a tractor-trailer on the spot and become this century's first great hay baron.

I keep waiting for Detroit to start coming out with more hay-efficient animals, but until they do, we are forced to turn to conservation.

We used to just toss a flake of hay on the ground, but this is wasteful. The goats and alpacas in particular will eat some of the hay, but they will also play with it, paw at it, roll in it and sleep in it. As a kid, I heard the term, "Don't play with your food," but I never thought it would one day apply to camelids.

Anyway, to promote efficiency, I bolted a hay feeder to the goat pen and informed Beth of my plans to build a hay feeder for the four alpacas. I floated the idea as a money saver, although privately I was thinking that an actual feeder would cut down on the number of hay rounds we had to make each day, and hence the amount of labor I personally need to invest. (That little scheme didn't work, but never mind for now).

Problem was, I now had to buy some lumber and actually build the thing. And, long story short, construction is not my strength. I hear carpenters say stuff like "measure twice, cut once," but that seemed like a lot of bother, so I'd cut twice as much as needed, never measuring at all, on the theory that one piece of stock or another would at least come close to fitting.

This always resulted in finished products that were not terribly functional but were unspeakably picturesque.

Luckily for me, the feeder plans were not complicated: a few two-by-fours nailed in the shape of a hay bale. Beth really shouldn't have said anything, but like all loyal wives, she saw a need to "boost my confidence" by making the project sound as if I'd just built a three-story beach house.

"Wooowwww. That's really impressive. I am so proud of you." It was the same tone she used on Opie the first time he managed not to go to the bathroom in the house. The miracle was that she stopped before telling me, "You're such a big boy today."

"Thanks," I said. "That and $6 will get you a bale of hay."

Seven-Month Old Canine Comedian Thinks Everything is Funny

Never hold a chocolate-chip cookie in one hand and a dog biscuit in the other.

I don't want to get into any details — but it can get confusing, is all.

Treats are necessary to encourage the Bouvier de Flandres named Opie to do anything these days. The puppy is about 60 pounds and seven months old, which in dog years means he's about 5.

But he's showing all the symptoms of being a teenager, in that he has reached the age where he will do nothing unless he judges there is something in it for him.

Worse, and I suppose some would consider this to be poetic justice, he has turned out to be the world's biggest canine comedian.

He thinks everything is funny.

When he's racing the bulldog Hannah up the stairs, he loves to "put her into the wall," like a NASCAR driver. When he sees Hannah ambling toward the couch, he'll race across the room and dive up on it just ahead of her, then lie there with this great big grin on his face.

The whole world is a joke. Now I know why so many people can't stand me.

His favorite game is to sneak his toys out-of-doors, which Beth doesn't allow for some reason. This sets off a Titanic battle of wills, complicated by the fact that the BDF's mouth is so big he can rather easily conceal anything up to the size of a set of luggage.

"Fine," Beth will say, as he's standing there with the remnants of what used to be a stuffed raccoon in his mouth. "Then you're staying in." And she'll shut the door and begin to walk away. Opie, in turn, his face dripping with fake remorse, will drop the toy and come to the door again, begging for forgiveness and access to the backyard.

"That's better," Beth will say, opening the door — at which point, Opie will bolt back, grab his toy and lunge for the porch, usually to find the door slammed back in his face until once again he drops the toy and petitions for freedom. Again, the door will open and, again, he snatches up the toy and flies at the door. This exercise will be repeated on the order of, oh, I don't know, perhaps 3 million times under the auspices of "it's the only way he'll learn."

Meanwhile I'm sitting out on the patio, idly pulling stink bugs out of my hat, hoping there will be some resolution between Beth and Bouvier some time before my knees need to be replaced.

Occasionally, Opie will succeed and slip through the rapidly narrowing door opening. Kings have not been as excited about acquiring the throne as Opie is at winning this game.

Once he has the toy outside, you might expect him to play with it, but he doesn't. He immediately spits out the shapeless, soggy, offending object and goes off to some other activity.

Clearly, the point wasn't that he wanted the toy, the point was a play a joke on mom.

Look at me. I got the toy out of the house. I am the most hilarious dog ever.

Conversely, sticks and walnuts are not allowed IN the house, for similarly vague reasons. This obviously sets off another round of gamesmanship that can go on to the point that 90 percent of our waking hours are basically spent trying to go in and out of the house.

Thinking he might benefit from some "real world" experience, we took Opie to the Humane Society's "Canines on the Canal" event in Williamsport over the weekend. You know, just to show him that most dogs do not fancy themselves as Groucho Marx.

But for once he was serious. Instead of playing his usual pranks, he spent his time networking — sniffing, exchanging dog business cards and the like. That can't be good.

If we all wake up some morning to discover the county's dogs have draped all our trees with tuggie toys, you'll know who to blame.

It worries me no end.

D-Requiem for a Dead Groundhog

The good news is that I got the groundhog.

The bad news is that I got the groundhog.

Two of them, actually, leaving only an estimated 24,998 left in the field.

I would have nothing against woodchucks as a species if they would stay in the woods where they belong, eating sumac and playing tip jars, or whatever it is they do for entertainment.

But they insist on invading my personal space, digging under barns and garden fences. They don't nibble like rabbits, they gorge. You get the sense they have a Martha Stewart element to them, and if each single bean plant in the row isn't chomped down to the exact same level it makes them uncomfortable in an artistic sense.

So something had to be done, and Beth knew exactly what it was. Next time we saw the fat little rodent gnawing on a sunflower she casually handed me a shotgun.

I have nothing against guns. If people want to own them it's fine with me. If they want to shoot people, I will be happy to provide a list of prospects.

But I'm not entirely comfortable with them, either. I don't appreciate loud noises, such as gunfire, jackhammers and Chris Matthews. Being the man, however, I couldn't look soft in front of the chick. So, with a manly swagger, I gripped the weapon in a manly fashion and — after a manly moment to figure out which end of the shell went into the chamber first — walked into the pasture with a manly quickness.

I slammed the round home. I cocked the cocky thingie. I aimed.

I — this is where it gets awkward.

It was much like the scene in "Animal House" where D-Day and Bluto hand Flounder the gun and tell him to shoot the horse. I closed my eyes, turned my head and fired in the general direction.

The result was a cloud of dust and an animal that seemed to realize that an occurrence had just transpired, but wasn't sure what. He rolled twice from the percussion, then picked himself up and dove into the woods.

Beth tried to console me: "Wow, good shot. I don't think I've ever seen a groundhog quite that scared."

Since it rolled, I maintained that I scored a hit. Dubious, Beth headed for the woods. I stopped her. "Don't do that; there's nothing more dangerous than a wounded groundhog."

Since the next day the groundhog, arm in a sling, was back under the apple tree munching fallen fruit, Plan B was a Hav-a-Heart trap. Quickly, we caught a youngster. The thought of opening the trap and shooting him didn't seem sporting somehow, so we relocated the beast to a nice mountain home. With views.

The next one, the surly, granddaddy, monster, "I will dig under the barn until it caves in" groundhog was not so easy. His crimes clearly warranted a death sentence. He was big. He was ugly. And he smelled.

Our friend Walter had offered to come over and dispatch any further catches, but he's a rugged, long-time farmer whom I am trying to impress. I can't have him thinking that I am a greenhorn — anymore than he already does.

Hannah the English bulldog, who was snarling outside the cage, seemed willing to offer her services as well. It should be noted here that Opie, the Bouvier des Flandres puppy is a very brave dog. But, by coincidence, the moment the BDF saw the wild, caged animal, he suddenly remembered a pressing engagement in the house, underneath the couch.

So, since we were on the way to the horse barn at the time, we decided to put the critter — the groundhog, not Opie — in the shed until our return.

Having decided to do what needed to be done, we got out of the car an hour or so later. I went for the shed and Beth went for the armory.

All it took was one glance.

"Uh, Beth? You don't have to worry quite so much about the gun."

Sure enough, he had expired on his own. And let that be a lesson to all of you who ignore those government warnings about overeating. He was so fat on our apples, he appeared to have a stroke.

Speaking of stroke — as in genius, of — I buried him in his own hole. Meanwhile I looked up to see Beth — and this is such a woman thing to do I can't stand it — cleaning the trap with paper towels and Windex.

Wouldn't want the next groundhog to be offended by his new surroundings.

A Sure-Fire Crow Cure: Kill 'Em All

Well, at least Southeast Asia listens to me. Three years ago I offered the city of Hagerstown this free advice for ridding itself of crows:

Shoot them.

Now, the New York Times reports that the island nation of Singapore has adopted this solution for ridding itself of unwanted crows:

Shoot them.

That's right, the city that brought us some humorous moments with its public canings and bans on chewing gum, has enlisted a get tough on **crows** policy that involves ranks of men with shotguns blasting away into the dusk.

This year, they figure they can kill 20,000 of Singapore's 100,000 crows.

"There is no bloodlust evident among the men, only a solemn respect for their foe's notorious cunning," the New York Times reports. "Social beings, crows will signal others of danger and organize to defend wounded fellows if possible. Marksmen swear the crows recognize guns on sight."

No bloodlust? Well where's the fun in that? Guns without bloodlust is like handball without a wall.

And when did crows become such noble beasts. Solemn respect?

Hello, Singapore. We're not talking about a Bengal Tiger here. These are flying vermin, winged rats. Don't treat it as if you're going to be mounting a crow head over your fireplace in the den.

And why is shooting crows, especially here in Hagerstown, more important than ever? Because I happen to have in my hands a press release from the Maryland Department of Health and Mental Fearmongering entitled "Maryland Crows Test Positive for West Nile Virus."

Gee. I hope they remembered to strip them of their Olympic golds.

The state is asking our help in finding out more about the scope of the virus: "Citizens are asked to call and report any dead or dying bird to the Maryland Department of Natural Resources' toll free hotline at 1-888-584-3110. Optimum specimens for testing are birds that have died within 24 hours prior to calling the hotline. Sunken or cloudy eyes and infested with fly larvae (maggots) are good indicators that the bird has been dead too long for testing."

Oh come now. Back where I come from in West Virginia, fly larvae is what puts the zip in the potpie.

Now that I've lived in Maryland a while though, I'm not certain I want to get close enough to a crow carcass to determine whether its eyes are sunken, or merely cloudy.

Of course there's one way to guarantee a good fresh crow carcass: Shoot them. Which is where I started out in the first place.

Back to the Singapore model, it's interesting to note that they award the shooting jobs to the city's banking and business elite.

The Times reports: "The sharpshooters arrived, 18 in all, not in rusted pickups with gun racks, but in BMWs and shiny new Japanese sedans. The club secretary, Tang Kee Khong, emerging from a vintage Mercedes, launched the attack."

Well, there you go. We can just fix up the guys over at Ferris, Baker, Watts with some Remingtons and let them go nuts.

There's your tourist attraction, Mayor. Come to Hagerstown and see the men in worsted wool suits marching up Antietam Street blowing away blackbirds.

It would be the next best thing to giving them a public caning.

Some Day You Might Get to Say, I Want My Steak Medium Stupid

To some degree or another, I believe all of us are concerned with the conditions in which farm animals are raised.

Cramped, restrictive and pathetic environments can't be much fun, even for creatures that are not equipped with human intellect and awareness. You know, chickens in cages, hogs in pens, calves in crates, Rosie O'Donnell in "The View."

Even sworn meat eaters are likely to be a little uneasy about the agribusiness tactics of confinement that render the steak tender. So most of us, instead of giving up the lamb chops, choose simply not to think about it. If you like barbecue, you simply can't be concerned about whether or not the donor grew up depressed.

But for all the caring carnivores out there, I have great news. Science is about to solve the problem.

No, science has not figured out a way to allow animals to romp and play on the range while remaining fork-tender. Instead, it's addressing the problem from the other end.

Animals will remain caged in ridiculously cramped quarters. But they'll be genetically engineered so they will be too ignorant to realize they're being mistreated.

How brilliant is that?

"Scientists are actively investigating ways to remove the stress and aggression gene from animals, effectively turning them into complacent zombies," writes the London Daily Mail.

Scientists say "it might become technically possible to produce 'animal vegetables' — beasts which are 'highly prolific and oblivious to their physical and mental status.'"

A little Prozac for your pork chop.

"Sir, how would you like your steak?"

"Medium stupid."

Talk about staying one step ahead of PETA. Who can argue about a brain-dead lump of protoplasm that does nothing but expand until it has a tenderloin the size of a love seat?

All this time, science fiction has been ginning up fears that genetic engineering could lead to animals that are super-smart. Who knew it would be the other way around?

Cramped cages? They won't even need cages. The rooster won't be able to figure out that by putting one foot in front of another he can actually get somewhere.

Who needs free-range chickens when you have special-needs chickens? You don't go to the slaughterhouse in the cattle truck, you go in the short bus.

Whether this dumbing down of farm animals is necessary is hard to say. I raised chickens when I was a boy, and it's not like they spent their days shooting dice, or engaging any other entertainment more complex than making life miserable for the grubs.

It was a pretty basic social structure. The hens spent their days scratching for bugs and the roosters spent their days breaking each other's necks. I can't say I spent a lot of time thinking about their relative happiness, although some did seem to have borderline personalities.

How much of this was attributable to their native intelligence and how much was attributable to the fact that I had just shoveled out the coop and was overcome by fumes is difficult to say. But they seemed content enough, at least until we lopped off their melons.

And to my knowledge, no farmer I worked for ever thought about castrating the pigs and giving them a lobotomy while they were at it. The food chain was the food chain. At butchering time, you rounded up the hogs and life went on. Well, theirs didn't, but you get the drift.

It is hard to figure whether an animal would be happier by not knowing that it was unhappy. You walk through the veal pens and some genetically altered calf is standing there going "la-la-la, la-la-la" and maybe it makes you feel better about things, but I'm not so sure about the critter. And is it really necessary to go to all the trouble to genetically alter the cow into a stupor? Seems to me like you could just get it drunk.

Look, if knowing your hog was in a fog makes you feel better about eating spare ribs, then fine. But since they all end up the same way anyway — dead — what's the difference?

Youth is Valuable,
Even for Puppies

I never had any kids of my own, so I never knew the joys of watching a little tike learn to walk, talk, sign complex sub-prime mortgage lending documents, or any of those other joys that make parents wipe a tear from their eyes and say, "For this I missed a European vacation?"

So I have to take my pleasures of young life where I can find them — such as the day the bouvier de Flandres puppy named Opie learned to lift his leg. Yes, today he is a man.

All right, so it's not learning to ride a bike, but it's something, OK?

Frankly, I never knew that young, male dogs — when they had to water the tulips, so to speak — did not lift their legs from birth.

I feel so isolated. And it's something you just don't stop to think about. You never hear a co-worker say, "I need that report on my desk by tomorrow morning, and by the way, did you know that boy puppies shake the dew off the lily in the same manner as girl puppies until they are several months old?"

But it's true. And it seems that this represents some sort of milestone in male puppyhood. Beth, who had previous experience in these manners, ran breathlessly into the house the other day and exploded forth with a joyous, "Opie lifted his leg!"

"He which?"

"Lifted his leg; you know, like a big dog."

"Oooohhhh, he lifted his LEEGGG. Why that's just — just ..." Words failed me at that point. I felt as if I ought to do something like, I don't know, bake a cake. Or at least feel a little more excited about the event.

I mean, lifting their legs is kind of what dogs do. It's not like he divided pi or anything.

Besides, I rather felt bad for the pup. Because, if my life is any indication, lifting your leg (symbolically speaking, of course) is just the precursor to greater, and not always pleasanter, responsibilities.

Responsibilities of which Opie, as of now, has exactly zero. We try to correct him, but it's always a failure. You shake your finger at him, all he does is lick it. He will learn in time that a big dog that can lift his leg will be expected to perform other duties, such as refraining from grabbing one trailing end of the wisteria and running until the entire plant — trellis and all — follows him off into the distance.

When he has learned to lift his leg, he will certainly have to learn that not everything in life is a joke. For the Siamese cat named Juliet and the Bulldog named Hannah, this revelation cannot come soon enough.

These two animals are older and wiser and as older and wiser animals know, there is more to life than fun and games — most notably, sleep. Which, of course is out of the question when the BDF pup is going full Sandy Duncan, spreading his brand of energetic pixie dust throughout the house and yard. They want to sleep. They try to sleep. They have just gotten to sleep ... when 50 pounds of coiled spring lands squarely on their midsections, producing an exhalation of wind with an audible oomph. After which, Opie jumps in the air, whirls a 360, bobs his head and waves his paws at the great gag he's just pulled.

I had not previously, that I know of, seen a bulldog and a Siamese seriously contemplate murder. Now I have, and it's not pretty. Hatred, then indignation, then resignation drip from their eyes as they can tell that the youngster will not be disciplined until he's older — until he learns to lift his leg.

Which, as of this writing, Opie has stopped doing. To our knowledge, he only successfully mastered the exercise three times, and hasn't done it since. Maybe he senses something. Like he realizes his youth is too valuable to be lost for such trivial an accomplishment as an upwardly poised hindquarter.

I began to admire him. "You are right, Opie my boy," I told him. "Do not let your youth slip away easily. Hold to it with all your strength. Stay young. There is nothing so free as a puppy chasing butterflies, nothing so innocent as a warm tongue licking your cheek. Do not be quick to take on the burdens of the world, for it awaits all too soon with its troubles, as surely as the robin arrives in the sp ..."

At this point the dog named Opie threw up a hairball. Oh well.

Death to the Chickens

The grim headline was terrorizing, even to those steeled against the horrors of the world. It screamed "All Hong Kong Chickens Must Die."

See, I knew turning the city over to Communist China would come to no good. It always starts with chickens, doesn't it? Stalin started with chickens, sending thousands to the infamous gulag coops of the great north.

Television graphically showed men in white moon suits and gas masks, with ruthless efficiency stuffing chickens. And I'm not talking about stuffing them with apple walnut dressing. No, 1.3 million chickens, most of whom had been looking forward to a happy rendezvous with a wok, were being stuffed into trash bags and given a gaseous blast with the nite-nite nozzle.

Because of the avian flu virus known as A H5N1 (so-named because "mumps" was already taken), health officials called for the slaughter of all Hong Kong chickens, although what 1.3 million chickens are doing living in the city, I'd like to know.

The mass slaughter, they hope, will snuff out the disease, which is blamed for the death of four people and the sickening of a dozen or so more.

In the United States more people than that are gored to death by cattle each day, but you don't see us stuffing cows into trash bags.

Who does the Chinese premier think he is, the Pharaoh?

Maybe somewhere in the city a farmer has tucked a baby chick into a reed basket and hidden him in the bulrushes and 20 years from now this great chicken will part the Zhu River and lead the oppressed into the land of grubs and corn meal.

Hey, that's my idea! You put down that cell phone, Oliver Stone!

I don't see why they have to kill them. Couldn't they just shake the eggs? (Speaking of which, perhaps they could send some of these Chinese Avian Death Squads over here to deal with the geese at City Park.)

According to The Washington Post, "the biggest problem was that the number of workers deployed for the operation — 1,200 from the agriculture department — had no experience in handling, let alone killing, chickens. They are largely desk-bound bureaucrats, working in jobs such as licensing and transportation, looking after Hong Kong's country parks and supervising rabies cases."

Imagine. There's some hapless Chinese version of Dilbert sitting in front of his spreadsheet and someone comes up and hands him a gas mask and says, "Today's going to be a little different."

And Chinese restaurants were obviously feeling the anguish.

"You can still see chicken on the menu," a cashier at one of Hong Kong's premier restaurants told the Post. "But anything with two feet we don't have."

Look for the National Pig Council people to move in soon, with their "Pork: It's the Other Non-Viral White Meat" slogan and "easy substitute" recipes in which pork roasts are somehow made out to have drumsticks.

The real messy thing though is that dogs and rats are starting to dig up the mass chicken graves, and health officials are worried the virus will be transmitted to them. And while the American public may sit passionlessly by and watch chickens and rats be destroyed, what will they think if health officials have to start executing pups?

What to Do When Chased by a Wild Goose

Hagerstown has certainly had its go-rounds with geese, cataclysmic upheavals that I've always just sort of written off as Hagerstown being Hagerstown.

Every year at "City" Park there is some goose-related crisis that touches off endless meetings at City Hall entertaining ideas for reducing the goose population while avoiding the PR disaster of having PETA-types jumping down our throats faster than Cheese Doodles on a stoop-sitter.

Only here, I thought, would it be possible to have a protracted debate centering on the ethics of shaking goose eggs so they wouldn't hatch.

I didn't find that to be inhumane, I just worried that the eggs might not be shaken hard enough, and you might wind up hatching a bunch of geese that were merely brain damaged, which would leave taxpayers open to the liability of SSI payments.

But **geese**, it seems, are not simply a localized problem, and as evidence I turn to an Actual Memo to employees from the Columbus (Ohio) Dispatch facilities maintenance department.

It begins: "Spring is upon us and our waterfowl friends have again taken up residence for the 2007 season. It is very important for your personal safety that you understand some basic habits of this particular species during the nesting season."

Fair enough. There's a bit of a disconnect, in my view, between "friends" and having to look out for one's "personal safety," but they could be simply warning against stepping on eggs and slipping on the yolk. Explain that to the insurance adjuster.

But then the memo becomes darker:

"The female will begin laying eggs from mid March to early April; it is the female you will see tending the nest. The gander will normally be in the area and no more than 20 yards off. You must be alert and aware when walking to and from the building; the gander will attack you if it believes you are too close to the nesting female or pose a threat. This attack can come from any direction so take notice of any geese in the area that you see while walking."

Whew. You don't know whether they're talking about a corporate campus or a Nintendo video game. "Night of the Goose; the Flock Strikes Back."

Sounds as if just to get from the building to your car you need a pad of graph paper and a slide rule. Warning — 30 yards to car, 20 yards to goose. Engage evasive countermeasures. Coming to work every morning turns into "The Hunt for Red October."

To be fair, we are assured that, "The facilities maintenance staff, as in years past, will make every effort to limit any human-goose conflict situations by all legal means at our disposal."

Human-goose conflict situation. As any good SWAT team member can tell you, an HGCS is a serious deal. I have a friend who works at the Dispatch, and out of concern for her safety I dropped a note asking about the number of HGCS incidents a year.

She didn't know. Apparently the problem is not at the main newspaper office, but at the out-of-town print shop. "I've only been there three times in 17 years," she said.

Well I reckon so, if every trip puts you at risk of being clocked by Donald Duck. And that begs the point, if you are at risk of an HGCS, why must you remain in the realm of the "legal?" I don't care if it lands me 30 days, I'm taking a baseball bat.

But the memo says there are other solutions, including:

1. Maintain direct eye contact with the goose and face toward it.

2. If the goose acts aggressively, calmly and slowly back away.

3. Maintain a neutral demeanor, do not act hostile or show fear.

4. Never turn your back to an aggressive goose.

5. If a goose flies toward your face, duck and move at a right angle to the direction of flight while maintaining your front toward the goose.

Lessons for life. In reading it over, it struck me that men might even be able to strike the word "goose" and insert the word "wife" if things reached that stage.

We'd all be better off if we applied the rules of nature to our everyday lives.

Obedience School I

Opie goes to obedience school
A personal journey
Part I

We're in the training hall, 7-month-old, 70-pound Opie is in full freakout mode, lunging at his tether, I'm lunging at Opie, we both get tangled and end up on the floor, I'm told to start shoving treats in his face and I do and he throws them back up on my pants, he howls and groans and I'm looking around desperately for help and it finally arrives when the teachers decide that the only way to keep his heart attacks down to one a minute is to place visual barriers around his training station.

So — I thought the first day went well.

The bouvier de Flandres is getting to be a big boy, and at times I fear he outgrew his brain at about 5 months. So he definitely needed some schooling. Actually, this was our second class, but the first one went noticeably better because we were not required to bring our dogs. The school, Peaceable Paws, encourages a technique called "click and treat." The only equipment required is a small clicker and about seven pounds of food. Shirley, our instructor, said we would be amazed at how soon the animals would pick up on this — the dog learns that when he hears the click, something good happens and modifies his behavior accordingly.

Beth and I liked the idea because it trains based on rewards instead of punishment. And I couldn't believe how well it worked. At home, the BDF learned to sit the first day that I worked with him and he learned "down" on the second.

I'm not terribly competitive, but I am terribly proud of Opie and I worked with him quite a bit through the week to ensure he would be the star of the class. And if by "star," you mean "Bill O'Reilly-like meltdown," he didn't disappoint. He panicked. Then I panicked. Then we both panicked in one big panic volcano. He paid no attention to my voice. He paid no attention to my treats. He didn't want cheese, he didn't want a meatball, he didn't want grilled chicken breast. All he wanted was his mommy, who by that time was at the other end of the room with Hannah the bulldog, who is basically obedient, but was enrolled because we figured she could use a refresher course.

So there was everyone else in the hall, dogs neatly at their feet, sitting and downing and calm and happy — and then there was me and the Ope, off in a corner, behind three-foot barricades, lacking only the pointy dunce caps. At that very moment, I wanted nothing more than to be out of there, and Opie was seconding the motion.

It was Shirley who came to the rescue, talking sweetly to Opie and working him into a calmer frame of mind.

I was grateful, but I couldn't understand why Opie would listen to her and not me. On the drive home, Beth "put out a feeler" that perhaps I was part of the problem. I was dubious.

"He feeds off of you, and he can tell ..."

"Of course he feeds off me, I stuffed enough cheese in his face to keep Wisconsin in business for the next ..."

"... No, he's very attuned to you, and if you're scared, he'll pick up on that and he'll be ..."

"... No he won't, he's a dog, for heaven's ..."

"... Because he trusts you and he can sense when you ..."

"... He's a dog, Beth, a dog. Not Kreskin. A dog ..."

"... Panic and that makes him worry that ..."

"... No, he wasn't worried. Grandmothers worry. He went full Jamie Lee Curtis in 'Halloween II'..."

"... There might really be something to be afraid of."

I stopped talking, a move that usually plays out to be among the smartest things I ever do. Beth assures me that as he gets used to other dogs, he'll be happier, more attentive and better behaved.

As for me — well, it's a process.

Tundra Swans May Win by a Neck at City Park

I was spending a typical Thanksgiving morning sitting at home cleaning my guns, when I noticed a story in the holiday paper about the big birds.

No, not turkeys. Swans.

Apparently there's trouble brewin' over which breed of swan will be introduced — or reintroduced — to the lake at the creatively named City Park.

The city wants Mute Swans. The State of Maryland wants Tundra Swans.

Let me explain the difference.

Actually, I'm not sure I can explain the difference. If I have my facts straight, which admittedly would be breaking new ground in this space, the Mute Swans are more swanish, in that they have curved necks and are what we were accustomed to seeing at the park over the decades.

Tundra swans have straight necks, and the Department of Natural Resources strongly prefers them because they do not exhibit the personality flaws of the Mute variety.

The state says Mute Swans are obnoxious, pointlessly aggressive and tend to be out-of-control breeders. Sort of like a cross between Chris Matthews and Old Mother Hubbard.

The story says "A feral population of about 4,000 Mute Swans has caused problems for people and wildlife on Maryland's Eastern Shore."

They terrorize other birds, ripping up vegetation, eating their food and snapping at anyone who dares approach. To hear the state tell it, these swans have awful dispositions and take over areas in which they are not welcome. A couple of these lawless creatures have even been caught trying to vote. Well, not vote maybe, but at least conducting exit polls.

Along with the curved neck, you can tell them by their beards and turbans.

The thought of an "aggressive swan" reminds me of the bunny in Monty Python's "Search for the Holy Grail." I can envision City Park with a beautiful, graceful swan walking placidly amidst a broad scattering of men's bones.

The Tundra Swans are more peaceable and, the DNR says, "typically migrate through Maryland."

You've seen them, right? You'll be out on a crisp November morning and see a big ole flock of swans settling down to lunch in a cornfield on their way to Orlando.

I'm afraid this is one debate I have trouble joining. On one hand, I don't see what the big deal is over a neck. Are these birds or beer bottles? If a curvaceous neck is so important, why don't we get the Tundra Swans and bind their necks in an S shape like the Chinese did with women's feet?

On the other hand, the city had Mute Swans for years. I have spent a lot of time in the park and cannot once remember being held up by a swan at gunpoint. And the problem isn't that they kept multiplying, it's that they kept dying.

No doubt before this is all said and done in this dispute we'll be visited by about 4,000 feral lawyers duking it out in court over a couple of decorative waterfowl.

What is it about this city and birds? Whether it's shaking goose eggs or hosing off crows with grape Kool-Aid, there's always a surreal avian subplot running through Hagerstown.

I say we let the swans decide. Get one pair of Tundra and one pair of Mute and may the better swans win. There's Biblical precedent for either side. The evil Cain/Mute swan may slay the gentle Able/Tundra swan, but then again the virtuous David/Tundra swan might just up and surprise us by slaying the bellicose Goliath/Mute swan.

Either way, there would be a whole lot of slayin' going on and that, needless to say, has tourism potential. I'd set if for next June. Come to City Park for the 2002 Western Maryland Blues Fest/Swan Death Match. I'd like to see some other festival-happy city copy that.

City Cat Fights Resemble Groundhog Day

We're used to City Hall fighting like cats, but not fighting about cats. I get a warm feeling knowing there's always hope for breaking new ground.

In fairness, I don't know that the city was actually fighting about cats, more like discussing what should be done with a feral cat colony at City Park. But the phrase "We're used to City Hall discussing like cats..." doesn't work.

I am a professional, and I know these things.

The cats are taking the fall for an infestation of fleas at the grand old Mansion House art gallery, prompting some to urge that they be catnapped by the humane society.

That prompting prompted others to protest, saying that the pre-ferred course is something they call "cat management."

So we may have to get a group of feral lawyers in here to sort the mess out.

First of all, I have to live with a cat named Colonel Sanders. And I believe that gives me the expertise to suggest that the term "cat man-agement" is an oxymoron if ever there was one.

You want to manage a gang of cats? Good luck with that.

The theory goes that if you sweep all the lawless cats out of com-mon ground, the success will be short-lived because a new gang of lawless cats will move in. I believe the FBI had the same problems in Chicago.

The better plan, supposedly, is to pluck out the cats a few at a time for a quick trip through the EZ Spay express lane and then put them back. (Technically it's known as TNR, for Trap, Neuter and Release.) That way they don't reproduce, but they "protect their turf" against a more problematic influx of more fertile felines.

See how seamless it all is? Makes me wonder why we didn't put this much thought into our Iraq policy.

Maybe Rumsfeld should consider a TNR program for religious warlords. "Just chill M'abba, this will only take a second, and we'll have you back and car bombing in no time."

Thinking back a few years, wasn't everyone up in arms because City Park had too many birds? Now we have a lot of cats. So what's the problem?

Birds get out of hand, you get cats. Then if the cats get out of hand, we'll just introduce a bunch of dogs. If the dogs get out of hand we'll introduce badgers. Then wolves. Then lions. Then Teddy Roosevelt.

It all works out. So I guess I'm on board with the city, which pret-ty much decided to leave well enough alone.

But then there is still the original problem to deal with. Can't very well have the Mansion House turning into a flea market, can we?

There seems to be some dispute, however, over whether the fleas are being spread by cats or groundhogs. And I suppose you could turn the TNR program into the TNFCR (trap, neuter, flea collar, release) program.

If I'm a cat, yes, it's undignified, but it beats a one-way trip to Valley Proteins, if you know what I'm saying.

Hold on a minute. Did someone say groundhogs?

Boy, there's something you don't want to hear from the exterminator. "Sorry ma'am, you don't have box elders, you have — groundhogs."

I think someone's pulling our leg. This is sounding less like an animal control situation and more like a Monty Python situation: Woman calls the exterminator and finds out she doesn't have mice, she has sheep.

Myself, I'd deal with the groundhogs first. If your next arts event is a reading by P.G. Wodechuck, you've got to rearrange your priorities.

I had a groundhog problem a few years ago, which I mentioned in passing to a neighbor. Two days later, I swear, he shows up at my doorstep with this arsenal of smoke-emitting bombs and projectiles that would make the Suns fireworks look like a Reo Snapper.

Figuring if a little was good, more was better, I lit about 10 of them, chucked them down the groundhog hole, slammed a rock over it and dove behind the shrubs.

What I didn't know was that you can't just cover the main entrance, you have to cover all the entrances. Pretty soon thick columns of smoke were shooting up from about 20 spots throughout the entire neighborhood and for a second people thought they were going to have to call in Red Adair.

Caused quite a stir. Unfortunately, I had picked a time when everyone was home — except the groundhog. He was back eating my peas the next morning.

Obedience School II

Opie Goes to Obedience School
A Personal Journey
Part II

There's a Far Side cartoon that shows a dude in hell pushing a wheelbarrow of coal through the flames, whistling and having a grand old time. One devil looks at another and says, "You know, we're just not reaching that guy."

That's how I feel about the bouvier des Flandres named Opie. There's a smart dog in there somewhere, I know it. But his genius is tainted by youthful cackling and exuberance to the point that his skills become progressively more difficult to recognize.

I'm sure Mozart had days like that, too.

To date, Opie has learned "sit," "down," "touch" (where he plants his nose on your hand wherever you hold it — for reasons that are at the moment foggy), "leave it" and, if he's in the mood, "shake."

Well and good. Thing is, he knows he will get a treat if he performs one of these stunts, and little it matters to him which it is. So I take him out to the back porch to train him and he — as soon as he sees the treats and knows what's up — will go through the whole salad bar, knowing that something will be bound to trigger a hit.

I say, "Opie, sit." He proceeds to sit, lie down, touch my hand, picks up a toy and drops it and offers his paw. In his tiny little brain, he knows "sit" must mean one of these things, and even if he's not sure which, he wants to "cover his bases" in the name of a piece of cheese.

It's kind of being like a union member. Adhere to the "work rules" and you will get the benefit, whether you've earned it or not.

So do I give him the treat? Technically, he did sit. And for all I know, he is actually Edgar Cayce coming back as a hound, and he's successfully anticipated all the things I'm going to ask in the future, so he's just saving me the work — in which case, in theory, I should give him five treats and be done with the lesson.

Or not. Usually, it is the animal, not the trainer, who is supposed to be confused, but with Opie it doesn't work that way.

And frankly, getting the BDF to do something has never been the problem. Getting him to STOP doing things is the greater issue. They don't call them "Bouncing Bouviers" for nothing, and he thinks it's great fun to leap up repeatedly, grabbing a chunk of sweater or ear or whatever is handy, with each bounce.

Back in the days when he was only 50 pounds, this was rather cute. Now, I can't walk out to the barn without feeling as if I'm getting hit with a bag of cement with every step. A bag of cement with teeth.

Our training program stresses "positive reinforcement" and last week we were given a white paper outlining the negative aspects of punishment as a training tool. Dogs that are hit can become dull and listless, the paper says.

Dull? I dream of dull. Listless? I wish. Punishment doesn't work with Opie, because for him, there is no such thing as punishment. He thinks getting clubbed in the melon with a water bottle is the greatest game ever. Nothing makes him happier than to get smacked in the puss with a corn cob, mid-leap. He dances, runs in circles and then launches himself right back at you with pure canine joy.

I have one of these Fat-T-Boy reclining lounge chairs. Last night, I sank heavily into it, not realizing that one, the dog was at that time walking in front of the chair and two, that the footrest was not in its locked, down position.

The footrest snapped up like a catapult, catching Opie in the mid-section and launching him airborne across the room, where he crash-landed into the TV stand. I was sure I'd killed him, or at least broken three or four ribs.

He gave me one disbelieving look before flying back at the chair with twice the velocity at which he had been ejected, with the look of "WOW, that was FUN, let's do it AGAIN!"

You get the picture of why this is a challenging animal to train.

Swedish Study Proves it's Time for Animals to Step Off the Gas

If you have ever wondered how much a cow burps during the course of a day, you are not alone. You should be— as in padded-cell alone — but you are not.

For company, you have Swedish University, which just received a $590,000 grant to "measure the greenhouse gases released when cows belch," according to the Associated Press.

This is depressing. It shows just far we have fallen under the failed Bush presidency. It is a sad day indeed when other nations of the world pass the United States in the never-ending quest to pass out federal cash for frivolous studies.

It's not news that cattle produce methane, although we've usually thought of it coming at the other end of the spectrum, so to speak. But the Swedes say that "95 percent of the methane released by cows comes out through the mouth."

So about 20 cows (who's going to lead that cattle drive, Wyatt Urp?) will be fed varying diets and wear a special collar to measure the methane production.

The purpose of this study isn't clearly stated. Are they going the alternate-energy-source route or the cutback-on-harmful-emissions route? What if it comes down to a matter of destroying all of the cows in order to save the planet from coastal flooding? I know where I stand. I can do without New York City before I can do without New York Strip.

And if the cattle are that large a contributor to greenhouse gases, maybe the animals can be fitted with cowtalytic converters.

But seriously.

Hopefully, Swedish University will not find out about the bouvier des Flandres named Opie who, sad to say, is about 30 percent dog and 70 percent frat boy.

As is the case with many males, he thinks the standard belch is just about the funniest thing that has ever been invented for man or beast. After a meal, he'll jog happily over to the dainty Siamese cat Juliet, get right in her face and let rip with a healthy "Rrourrp."

Juliet, a princess among cats, will squeeze her eyes to slits and stalk off, viewing the dog with even more disgust than usual. Which, of course, is the point. Opie will prance, toss his head and laugh, ha ha ha, at his primitive little joke, only inspired by the fact that we, laughing through our teeth, are telling him "bad dog."

The animal also is encouraged by the fact that occasionally, not often, but once in a great, great while, I will — practically never, you understand — issue forth with an esophageal eructation of my own.

Opie loves this because he sees it as a male, human/canine bond of some sick sort. Again, he will toss his head and laugh, ho ho ho, and prance around the room with an unmistakable, "good one, dad," countenance.

Then, he will try to match it with one of his own, and turn an already sorry state of affairs up a notch with this game of his known as "belch tag" in which he will run up, burp on someone and run off, expecting the victim to try to chase him down and return the favor.

When I can bear to reflect on this at all — that here, a grown 47-year-old man could possibly find himself mixed up in a belching contest with a dog — it darkens my mood considerably.

Were it just a once-in-a-while occurrence, it might be tolerable. It might even be cute. But it happens with such frequency that I expect that at any moment, Opie might get a visit from Al Gore.

Hannah the bulldog stays out of it as much as she can, but then she has her own issues. Bulldogs, I have learned, are blessed with what is charitably known as "an active digestive tract," which is code for the unpleasant fact that their owners are routinely enveloped with bilious clouds of mustard gas that would have brought the British to their knees at the Hindenburg Line.

It's quite a one-two methane punch, all told. I don't need a Swedish study to tell me that if the ice caps melt, it is probably all my fault.

Animals Exhibit Worst Human Traits

If you stumble across an animal that doesn't eat in the winter, let me know. I'm not talking about a dog, cat, Hannah Montana or anything else that, for the most part, takes its feed indoors. I mean the big kind. The sort that eats out in the cold.

On milder days, there's a certain romance to taking the alpacas, donkeys, goats and geese a flake of hay or a scoop of grain as the sun is peeking over the hills and then again as it's disappearing with an orange glow in the west. But this romance approaches trial separation when the mercury hits 30; and below 20, we're talking nasty divorce.

Beth is philosophic: "It's the cycle of nature." I'm pragmatic: "It's freaking cold."

All right, back up a bit. I suppose I knew that farm animals ate during the winter. And I suppose I knew that they would not be able to make do on pasture all winter, hence the need for supplements. And I suppose that it's true that I have even gotten used to toting hay and water at the crack of dark in frigid temperatures.

But what I was totally unprepared for is the fact that the animals could be so — so human about it.

They all have this "me first" attitude that I always assumed was beneath the stoic donkey or the laid-back goat. And when they want their grub, they are capable of the most otherworldly noises imaginable.

Beth's late brother said they ought to make an alarm clock that sounded like a dog getting ready to throw up. While he might sleep through a tweet or a beep, the heaving "oork, oork, oork" of a pre-pukescent hound would have him wide awake in a flash, as he scrambled for a newspaper to shove under the muzzle.

Donkeys are much the same. I don't know who invented the word "heehaw," but that isn't what donkeys do — at least not Becky and Nelson. Maybe "heehaw" is a fallback, because there's no way to describe the actual article.

It might start with a "hee," or a reasonable facsimile. But this is just the single note on the piano to set the pitch for the full chorus. This note, which heralds the morning's first gray light, is roundly followed up with the most psychotic, murderous cacophony of piercing, screeching phonetics that resembles the air coming out of the world's largest and rustiest hinge.

Since the squeaky wheel gets the grease, this means the donkeys get fed first. Or they would, if we didn't have to pass the alpaca paddock on the way to the donkeys. The alpacas use the opposite strategy. While the donkeys make ugly, the alpacas bat their big, brown eyes and hum. It is impossible to pass them by with food destined for another animal.

Meanwhile, the goats counter by bleating and looking forlorn. Go ahead, feed everybody else first, that's OK with us, we'll just starve. Say a kind word at our funerals.

The geese aren't confined by fences, so they are free to follow in our footsteps, hacking and hissing at us. That's what geese do. You yell at them, they hiss. The dogs come near, they hiss. Feed them, they hiss. Buy them a diamond pendant and they would hiss. They are kind of like Randy Moss. But in a small way, I appreciate the consistency.

They're angry. I'm angry. But everyone gets fed, and all is right with the world.

Obedience School III

Opie Goes to Obedience School
A Personal Journey
Part III

We have time to think about our dogs, what, maybe three hours a day? Conversely, a dog has little else to do in the average work week than gnaw rawhide and think about us.

Those odds aren't good, but it's never been of particular concern before, since in the past all my dogs have had the equivalent of cotton candy between the ears.

I am thinking specifically of Lacie, who once was chasing a fox out at the college when it performed the highly elusive maneuver of going up a tree. Lacie, of course, did not notice and continued to chase air for the next three miles.

If any of these dogs needed to stand in for Lassie, little Timmy would have been mulch.

But an odd phenomenon has occurred. It appears that the bouvier des Flandres named Opie might actually be, dare I say, not stupid. Either that, or this is a really good obedience school because he is actually learning some beneficial behaviors.

This might or might not be good news because I want a dog that is smart, but not too smart, as in smarter than me. As mentioned, the BDF has a lot of time all day to sit around and think up ways in which his newfound knowledge can be put to use — for his benefit, not mine.

For example, he has been taught to "give," meaning that he will surrender whatever happens to be in his mouth at the time — toys, chews, small children — in exchange for praise or a treat.

He also knows that he has "indoor toys" that are not allowed to go out. So when it's time to go outside in the morning, he will dutifully grab an inside toy and stand at the door, knowing that he will be asked to "give." And when he does, he will be rewarded.

This has led Beth to speculate as to who is training whom. It's led me to accuse him of extortion.

After the last class, we went to a Christmas open house — explaining that we were late because we had just been to obedience training. Our friend Charlie looked at Beth and then nodded in my direction and asked her, "Is he learning anything?"

There was a dismal plausibility about this question because more and more I am finding myself behind Opie in the learning curve. Instead of owner being impatient with dog, dog gets impatient with owner — like I'm not getting it fast enough for him.

Along with one of his classmates, a border collie named Roxanne, Opie is possessed with what I call Alan Greenspan syndrome, seeing as both are blessed with a goodly portion of "irrational exuberance." They are happy, energetic dogs, eager to learn and keen on doing everything at once.

For example, during the lesson on "come," if Roxanne can streak toward her owner and midway leap up and grab something from the treat table and continue on without missing a stride — well, why wouldn't she?

The dogs are taught to run along what Shirley at Peaceable Paws calls "temptation alley," a minefield of canine temptations that they are — ideally — trained to ignore.

Opie can walk past the toy squid without interest. He can bypass the tennis ball, the tug toy and even a plate of dog food with nary a tug on his leash. But when he gets to the cow hoof, it's too much. It is like waving a martini in front of Dean Martin.

It's interesting to see each individual dog's weakness. Hannah the bulldog wanted the squid. Roxanne wanted the food. We are instructed to hold onto their leashes, keeping their noses a few inches away from the goodies, giving them a treat when they finally stop straining.

This usually works. Except in Roxanne's case, where — finding her progress impeded with her nose a few inches from the dog food said, "no problem," and simply reached out with her paw, instead of going to the food, pulled the food to her.

Next week is graduation and a competition to see whose dog has learned the most. The smart money is on Roxanne. But I think Opie would have a genuine shot were it not for me hanging around his neck like the millstone that I am.

Internet Hunting Lets Your Mouse Bag an Elephant

For our first stop in today's installment of "Animals in the News," we will visit a little place I like to call "Cyberspace," where a gentleman who is clearly ahead of his time has cooked up an idea that the rest of the country simply isn't ready for yet.

Basically, it's called Internet hunting, and allows a sporting chap the chance to aim, shoot and fire a real gun at real big game on his computer screen from hundreds or even thousands of miles away. Look, we've always heard that an elephant is scared of a mouse, and now Dumbo and Co. have good reason.

As I understand it, this is the brainchild of some dude in Texas (naturally) who has a ranch full of game that the paying customer can shoot by using a camera and gun mounted somewhere on the range, which he controls through his computer.

I absolutely love the idea of turning a nation of computer nerds into bloodthirsty killers, but it would seem that I am in the minority. Lawmakers in a number of states are falling all over themselves, trying to figure out which they want to ban first, Internet hunting or gay marriage. It is possible one or two states will become confused and outlaw gay hunters.

Even — and I find this hard to believe — the National Rifle Association is against the idea. My goodness, the NRA has gone soft? Come on, if guns that are controlled remotely by some unseen hand are outlawed, only outlaws will have guns that are controlled remotely by some unseen hand.

And the Constitution aside, I would think that Internet hunting would be such a time saver. I mean, who has time to get all dolled up in camouflage, buy some ammo, pack a lunch and head off to the forest anymore? Today's modern hunter is expected to be some kind of "superhunter," holding down a job, taking the kids to soccer practice, buying groceries, cooking dinner, cleaning house and blowing away Bambi all at the same time. It just can't be done.

With Internet hunting, it's boot up, log in, scroll over, scroll down, click-click, bang-bang, game over, in and out in 19 seconds, thanks for playing, we'll send you the head on a plaque, FedEx will have it to you on the third business day.

Is that so wrong? It's more humane, too, I think. Animal never knows what hits it. It never has to stare with fear into the eyes of its killer.

Besides, only the stupidest animal is not going to notice after a couple of days that a Very Bad Thing happens to any critter that walks in front of the camera with the antenna on it.

The bighorn sheep are going to be talking: "Hey Irving, I don't want to nag, but if I were you, I'd keep away from the one-eyed caribou over there on the platform."

And speaking of nag, that takes us to our next stop on the "Animals in the News" tour, Charles Town, W.Va., where last week owners of the Charles Town Races and Slots slapped a quarantine on their stables to try to head off an outbreak of equine herpes that was spreading among Maryland racehorses.

I had heard that Maryland horses were fast, but I had no idea. 'Course I didn't know there was any such thing as equine herpes either — or that Charles Town Races still has horses, for that matter.

Charles Town said its horses were, to date, disease free, and the quarantine was an attempt to keep it that way. No doubt. Don't want the place turning into another Mustang Ranch. It could be the end of maiden races as we know them.

Equine herpes would, however, be a good name for a horse. "As they come around the final turn into the home stretch, it's Equine Herpes by a half, with Mono y Mono on the rail and Elvirus closing fast on the outside..."

According to press accounts, equine herpes is known as EHV-1 and, like its cousin MTV, it can attack the central nervous system, causing mind-numbing paralysis. As a precaution, no horses from other tracks were allowed to come into Charles Town and those that left the track to race elsewhere could not return. Other horses are checked at the door.

When I am old, there will be some things I will be proud to say I have never done. One is working in retail. Another is checking out a horse for a venereal disease. No sir. Even if it could be done over the Internet.

A Mid-Horse Crisis

Against my better judgment, I have enrolled in horse-riding classes.

You do these things when, for one reason or another, you start your life over. Mine was a forced restart and not my idea, but it is working out for the best because after too many years of waiting it is finally allowing me to proceed with my god-given right to a mid-life crisis.

Except that mid-life doesn't seem quite long enough for a crisis. Sports car, trophy broad, two years tops then you flame out and go back to clock punching and couch warming for the rest of your life.

What fun is that? No, I'm shooting for a mid-to-the-time-that-I-lose-all-my-teeth-life crisis.

Enter Tanner. Tanner is half thoroughbred, half draft horse. He's bigger than Brando and faster than Joan Collins. He's owned by some breeders in Frederick, Md, who — I mean to say they breed horses, not to imply that ... oh never mind — are teaching me the ropes.

I need the human intervention because Tanner is a nice enough horse but as training goes, he, left to his own devices, would tend to leave out a few steps. My first time out, Tanner assumed the instruction should go something like this: Lesson 1: Get on the horse. Lesson 2: Go from 0-60 in three seconds flat in a full bore, heels to the sky, hellbent for leather gallop.

I closed my eyes, grabbed his main like a vice and felt around for the ejector seat. Not that this would have really been necessary, as Tanner was in the process of performing an admirable ejection on his own. Fortunately Tommy, my instructor, stepped in at this moment and reminded the animal that a horse has to walk before it can fly. After that, Tanner strolled along quietly enough, although clearly preoccupied. This worried me a bit, as I thought he might be plotting out some other experiment to try out on the new meat.

But I was afforded enough time to learn to walk and steer. I don't think "steer" is the generally accepted horse word for it, but I was concentrating on too many other things to be working on expanding my vocabulary.

"The key," Tommy said, "is to keep the horse between you and the ground. I was all for that.

We commenced from walking to trotting and something that is known as "posting." Having four legs, a trotting horse goes up-down, up-down, up-down, up-down. Posting is the means by which the rider partially stands in the saddle two beats, thus eliminating the pounding of two of the up-downs. Ergo, up-down, up-down, up-down, up-down becomes up-down, up-down. If you are a woman, eliminating half of the up-down pounding is important, but if you are a man it is VERY important if you know what I mean.

Our first day's lesson concluded with me not getting it. I had it backward, going up on the downs and down on the ups. This made for roughly eight violent blue jean/leather collisions every 10 seconds.

But I haven't been defeated yet; I signed up for another lesson.

And when as I was leaving, Tommy paid me a compliment. Of all the riders he had ever coached, he said I dismounted with the fastest time on record.

Warming Up to the Brooder Clan

I'm reminded of the old salt telling the tale of a shipwreck that claimed 129 lives. He spun a marvelous tale of a raging gale at night, the heroic but vain effort of the crew and the ultimate result of 120 souls going to a watery grave. A member of the audience caught the discrepancy: "Wait, 120? I thought you said 129 lives were lost."

To which the salt replied, "The ship's cat drowned, too."

So when I say the population of Little Farm by the Creek doubled this week, it's a little dishonest in that the 19 new members of the clan now occupy a 3-foot-square box. Or brooder, as it's known in the business.

No farm is complete without a flock of chickens pecking and scratching about, so we decided to take the plunge for artistic purposes as much as anything else, and if they have a mind to lay a few eggs in the process, so much the better.

It needs to be said upfront that Beth and I have very different ideas about animal husbandry. Had it just been me, I would have ordered the chicks and then forgotten about them until a call came from the post office begging for relief from the incessant peeping. Then I would have thrown them in a cardboard box, turned on a desk lamp and said, "Ladies, you're on your own."

Beth, on the other hand, is an enlightened woman of science. She began by purchasing an estimated 27 books on raising chickens and devouring every word. So thoroughly did she immerse herself in poultry knowledge that I told her if she read one more paragraph, she'd probably be able to lay eggs herself.

Many human pregnancies have come and gone with less planning, research, nursery preparation and "test runs" of the chicks' arrival. That our chicken coop does not at this moment have a teddy bear mobile hanging from the ceiling for the little ones to stare at is probably only the product of the rare occurrence of me being able to keep my mouth shut.

And barriers against predators? Humph. If the Confederates had been in possession of an equal number of defenses at Cold Harbor, McDonald's today would be serving McCollards.

Of course, were it totally up to me, it's doubtful any of the chicks would have survived the first night.

Rather than the desk lamp I used when I raised chicks as a kid, we had two aluminum, professional-looking heat lamps to bring the brooder to the required 95 degrees. Now to Beth, 95 degrees is 95 degrees — not 94, not 96 — 95. But I took 95 to be a "suggested" temperature, and reckoned anything from 68 on up would be sufficient. At least I did at first. But pretty soon the male competitive gene overrode the male who-cares gene and I decided I would get the brooder to 95 or die.

The lamps were on chains hanging from the ceiling, and they are not precise instruments. Too high and the brooder chilled to 75 degrees. We compensated by lowering them five links each and the temperature skyrocketed to 120.

We were to the point of raising the left one three links, while lowering the right one two links and such before finally deciding that on average it was "close enough for blues" and if the chicks didn't like it, they were free to sign a petition.

So anyway, they're here and doing fine, peeping to beat the band, and scurrying all about and creating quite a show and - have I ever mentioned that we have a bouvier des Flandres named Opie? Just in passing, I should mention that if you ever want to see a pup suffer five simultaneous heart attacks, just show him a brooder full of chicks.

Long story short, heat in the brooder is no longer an issue.

Obedience School IV

Opie goes to obedience school.
A personal journey; conclusion, sort of.

When someone has all the promise in the world, all the talent, all the goods, and then throws it to the wind, it is always a time of sadness. All one can do is shake his head at what might have been.

The bouvier des Flandres named Opie was primed to excel as we walked into his graduation day competition at Peaceable Paws. He had come a million miles since his first class, when he was so hyper and out of his mind with unreasonable excitement that he went full TV weather girl and had to have visual barriers placed around his person so as to put the brakes on overstimulation.

Since that time, he had adjusted, learned to associate with other dogs and stopped spinning crazily around the classroom like a finless missile, for the most part. He's even learned a few things along the way. More than a few. Enough that I went in foolishly thinking that he had a puncher's chance to win these doggie Olympics.

And he choked, like a choking dog — except in this case, he really is a choking dog. So much talent, and he only wound up with shameful bronze. Opie is the Michelle Kwan of the dog world.

As admitted last time, I confess to being part of the problem. For example, the handler is encouraged to gain the dog's attention by making "kissy noises." I am completely confident in my manhood, but I'll tell you this: It will be a cold day in hell when I start making "kissy noises" or anything resembling "kissy noises" to an animal in front of a room full of people.

Anyway, Opie dug himself a hole right off the bat in a competition called "puppy pushups," which frankly only is slightly to the north of "kissy noises" in terms of dignity. To complete a puppy pushup, the dog must sit on command, then go down on command. Then sit, then down and so on. Most pushups wins.

Opie responds to "sit" and "down." The problem is that when the dog stands up in between, it is viewed as a disqualification and the count begins anew. Well, keeping the BDF earthbound for more than a few seconds at a time is an art that has not been accomplished to date. If the rules had been: Sit, down, jump 4 feet off the ground, sit, down, jump 4 feet off the ground, we would have been golden.

As it was, Opie only strung together three pushups, and if we'd had a French judge, he probably wouldn't have been awarded those. Meanwhile, the beautiful border collie and eventual gold medalist Roxanne was doing 17. Even Beth's English bulldog Hannah — a dog that is built much like an aircraft carrier, although not as nimble — was able to nail five.

The pattern for the evening had been set. I could have stomached losing to Roxanne, but losing to Hannah ...

Hannah is like your own teenager. At home, he's surly, grumpy, foul-mouthed and nonresponsive, but get him out in public and he's the picture of charm and articulation and everyone says, "Oh, what a wonderful kid you have, he must be a joy to have around," and you think to yourself, "Humph."

Hannah Banana is like this. Basically moribund at home, you get her in front of an audience and she turns into Katie Freaking Couric. For her, there was the glory of second place, which she celebrated by promptly going home and falling asleep.

Opie did have some bright spots. But any though of a comeback was quashed when it came time to walk on a leash. Here's what a leash is to Opie: A toy given to a good dog to provide the entertainment of chewing it in half.

I have other issues as well. For example, during the competition, you got a point (called a bonus bone) if your dog went outside for a poo. I thought I'd have that one in the bag, so to speak — I had followed Opie around all evening trying to distract him so he wouldn't leave his bonus bone steaming in our backyard. But two seconds before we got in the truck, he hunched, with me there screaming, "No, no, NOOOO!"

Symbolic of the whole evening, as it turned out. But he did graduate and he received his diploma. Sort of like the scarecrow in "The Wizard of Oz," Beth said. So that means we can move on to Level II, if I have the strength.

Haircut Puts
Opie the Dog into a Tailspin

We didn't realize Opie was largely white. Opie didn't realize he was equipped with a tail.

You can learn so much from a haircut.

The bouvier des Flandres is now 9 months old, so in theory, he ought to be about fully grown. The fact that the animal kept expanding nonetheless was finally explained when we figured out that the inner dog may have maxed out, but the outer coat had not.

His sheepdog tendencies didn't bother me all that much, but then I don't clean the house. A desirable quality of the BDF is that he does not shed. An undesirable quality is that he counts among his hobbies the frequent roll in straw, dead leaves and sticks, all of which stick to his Velcro-like coat. When he would come in, all the compost would fall off through some freak of indoor humidity or something.

After Beth swept the kitchen floor to the point that the hardwood floorboards were wearing thin, she announced it was time for the dog to receive his first "big boy" haircut.

I looked at Opie. Opie looked at me.

For both of us, "big boy haircut" smacked of euphemism. Like when your boss tells you that you are to receive an "enhanced separation package" instead of directly saying you're fired.

But since Beth still had the broom in her hand, we both reckoned it was a good time to keep quiet, so we trundled off to Dogs R Us in Williamsport ("If your dog's not becoming to you, you should be coming to us"), where we placed Opie in Stephanie's able care.

It fell to me to retrieve the animal later that day, and for a split second I didn't recognize him. Stephanie is an artist, there is no other way to put it.

Opie looked so — so ...

I hate to use this word in the same sentence as "Opie" for fear the computer may crash, but he looked so *dignified*. Curiously, while his outer fur had been nearly all black, the undercoat was salt and pepper, like a mariner's beard. The shag had entirely camouflaged this fact. It had also camouflaged his stubby tail, which had never been introduced into evidence before.

Back home, Beth, Opie and I reverently reviewed the results. The old Opie was a big, shaggy goof. The new Opie appeared neat and trim and seemed a bit more serious. It was as if he realized he had passed into doghood. With this haircut, he knew, came responsibility. No more little boy. He looked the part, now he had to act it.

And that's when Opie first noticed the tail.

Because of all the fur, he had never known of its existence. Now, there was some foreign object affixed to his hindquarters that he didn't exactly like the looks of. And it was following him.

First, he tried to trot away from it, glancing back at his rump to see if it had been left behind. When it hadn't, he ran, then sprinted. But it was still there. Frantically, he called on evasive tactics, trying to ditch it. But after tearing multiple zig-zag paths though the yard in an effort to lose it, he was gassed and the tail had lost no ground whatsoever.

Fear crept into his eyes: "Yikes, it's as fast as me."

Unable to outrun it, he decided it had to be killed. To kill something, it must first be caught. But the cur was as agile as it was speedy. If you chased it to the left, it ran off to the right. Reversing the tactic reversed the result.

And the tail proved hard to sneak up on. The BDF would stand there for a while, casually enough, and then make one tremendous, mid-air 180-degree leap, hoping to catch it off-guard. But somehow, it always seemed to know what Opie had in mind. The spin would conclude with a mighty chomp, as the animal tried to bite the intruder in two. But by the time the teeth were where the tail had been, the tail was gone. A more puzzled, frustrated dog, you have never seen.

They exist under an uneasy truce at this time. Opie is still pretty sure that one day the tail will get overconfident and that's when he'll make his move. I'm pretty sure that once his hair grows back, he's likely to forget all about it. Opie is that kind of dog.

Tanner Takes the Lead

After four lessons, the score remains: Horse 4, Me 0.

Something tells me that in the old days of the Wild West cowboys never took riding lessons. Well, maybe they did in the form of basically being born on horseback. But I doubt anyone ever hollered at Billy the Kid, "Sit up straighter," "Keep an eye on the diagonal" and "More weight in the heels, Billy." Whatever, I'm sure it just came natural for them. For me it ain't natural.

The horse named Tanner hung with me for the first three lessons, and we were coming along OK until it came time to "canter." You learn to walk, trot, then canter, then who knows. Basically you are increasing in speeds from a pace that could merely break your arm to one that could leave your innards scattered across the width of Wyoming itself.

From a distance, cantering looks harmless enough, just as — seen from five miles below — it never looks as if a jet is going that fast. But when you are actually connected to the animal, cantering feels much as if you are riding the drumstick of a marching band member.

To go from a trot to a canter, you loosen the reins, dig in your heels and yell — prepare to be impressed with the precision of horse language — "canter." Except that Tanner seemed to be a bit behind in his vocabulary lessons, because he took "canter" to mean "buck." This was explained away with a wave of the hand and the comment that to him it "was a joke ... kind of a game." Whatever the game, I wasn't big on the rules. All the horses in the world, and I get Chris Rock.

Tanner would pitch me skyward and when I returned to earth, there would be open air where there used to be a horse. Keeping Tommy's mantra in mind — always keep the horse between you and the ground — I'd make a wild grab for anything solid — saddle, neck, passing tree, whatever. I always got seated again, feet out of the stirrups and facing backward as a general thing, but seated. After watching this spectacle a time or two, Tommy reckoned I could use a new model, so Tanner got traded in on "Cappy," a smaller animal that was less of a comedian.

First time out, we went on a "trail ride," which means following a path over hill and dale, up, over and around various obstacles. We were doing all right, avoiding low-lying limbs, descending steep swales and crossing small streams. It was a beautiful evening too, with a late sun filtering through the trees, and peace and a bit of haze in the air.

And that's when we first saw the snake.

Tommy helpfully pointed it out. A black snake it was, making up in size what it lacked in venom. I know black snakes are harmless, but that wasn't my concern. My concern was whether the horse knew they were harmless. For all I knew, Cappy had left her Field Guide to Reptiles in the barn. The horse didn't panic, but I did. I thought I was about to be dragged into the next county. But apparently the old cliché is flawed. Cappy couldn't have cared less. She gave it half an eye and walked on.

We followed it up with a nice canter, the proper kind, not the clown-inspired kind. I didn't even go airborne this time. I like this horse and am ready for the next lesson. At least I was, except that I could have sworn I heard Tommy say something about "jumping"...

One Cappuccino and I'm Back in the Saddle

It is possible to lease a horse, although I didn't know that before. There's still a lot I don't know, such as whether you have to pay 20 cents a mile if you exceed 12,000 in a year. And if so, is it possible to disconnect the horse's odometer?

The soon-to-be-leased animal in question is named Cappuccino, a mare that, as I understand it, is a cross between a draft horse and a thoroughbred and looks vaguely as if you had crossed Secretariat with Michael Moore.

Consequently, she's a mile high and runs like a California wildfire.

Truth be told, this wasn't really what I had bargained for when Beth (an expert dressage rider) signed me up for riding lessons. I had rather hoped for a small horse that I could straddle with my feet touching the ground, like training wheels. A slow horse. A tired, depressed horse. Maybe one with three legs. Something I could have a prayer of handling.

At first, I liked the sound of draft horse. I had draft horses figured as slow, plodding things, and with any luck maybe she would still be attached to the plow.

But the thoroughbred half of the equation spoiled that fantasy. You wouldn't think something that big could move that fast, but she does. First time I saw her run, the ground shook. Or maybe it was my knees.

"Learning to ride," my instructor Tommy said, "is simple. All you have to do is keep the horse between yourself and the ground." Fair enough. But Cappy is so tall, I don't know which was worrying me more, the prospect of falling or getting altitude sickness.

I thought back to when I was a boy, and all I ever wanted was a horse. And boots. And a hat and a big, western saddle with a lariat looped over the horn.

I get the idea that boys don't dream much of horses anymore. In fact, riding has turned into something of a pink-collar industry. Horse barns are filled with chicks.

In fact, Beth says that if a guy wants to meet a girl, one of the best ways is to get a horse. After six months riding, I would ask the guy this: "Just how bad to you want a girl?"

Truth be told, the riding part is great fun, especially since Cappy is well-trained and knows what to do even when I don't, which is to say most of the time.

And Tommy and Judy's Good Friday Farm is a beautiful, historic place to ride — trotting through wooded trails among white oaks with the falling leaves crunching underfoot, or cantering in big, open meadows as a setting sun reddens a sky filled with geese, and occasionally me, flying through the air.

Even the jumping has been OK, although I whined and complained that I would never be doing any jumping in "real life" and would prefer it if the horse had at least three feet on the ground at all times.

But the part of riding that gives me fits is all the out-of-saddle stuff — picking the hooves, brushing, washing and all the straps, belts and buckles involved. If one is looking for a reason horses are more popular with women, this is it.

It's the "women are better with knots" paradigm.

I can't figure out how to attach a bridle to save my life. To me, a bridle is a pasta bowl of leather straps that make no sense whatsoever. And forget all those buckles. Matter of fact, the first time I fell, it was because I had failed to adequately tighten the — and excuse me if I get a bit technical here — the strap thingie that holds the saddle onto the horse.

So I'm riding along fine until I notice that instead of being straight up and down, I'm about 20 degrees off plumb. Then 30 degrees, then 45, forming a definite right angle to the ground. This position is acceptable if you are an Arapaho Indian winging arrows at the sodbuster, but to a recreational rider, not so much.

Still, I'm hooked. If a horse can tolerate me, I should certainly be able to tolerate a horse.

Opie Gains Responsibility with Age

The bouvier de Flandres named Opie turns 1 year old this week, a fact of chronology that could not be proved by the fact of behavior.

In theory, he's not a puppy anymore, so he shouldn't be doing any of those kooky-crazy puppy things that include, but are not limited to, jousting with imaginary foes in the backyard and pulling up newly planted cherry trees.

We try to get through to him — we try to convey the gravitas that comes with being a full-grown dog. But it is no use. Other dogs have invisible fences around their yards; Opie has an invisible fence around his brain.

He has, however, figured out that grown-up dogs need to have grown-up-dog responsibilities, and he has two.

The first is the trash, which I totally don't get, because most dogs would rather get in it than guard it. Something, somewhere, somehow, planted the seed in Opie's head that garbage is a valuable commodity that needs to be protected from those who would do refuse ill. No one, and I mean NO ONE, is going to sneak in under the cover of night and try to slit the throat of our orange peels and coffee grounds.

Thursday is the most important day of the week for Opie, because this is Trash Day, the day I throw a bunch of bags and containers in the pickup and drive them to the road. He tears around the yard with religious elation, and heaven forbid I should ever drive the 200 yards to the road without him riding shotgun.

There, he assumes the most serious, determined expression that has ever shadowed the mug of a dog. I don't know who ferried around the Ark of the Covenant, but they couldn't have been any more steadfast than Opie when he's on task to get the trash to its destination.

Chugging back up the driveway, he always gives me a long, meaningful look: "We have done it. It was not easy — no one said it would be — but we have done it. We have taken out the garbage. Because we are men."

His other great responsibility, and this has happened in the last week, is the baby chicks. Again, no reason for it. You might think it would be the other way around. Indeed, Beth's dad, Wilson, believes Opie's preoccupation with the chicks might be less an article of protection than it is an article of diet.

But, I swear, there are days when Opie thinks he's a hen.

And the chicks love him right back. He'll stare into the brooder for as long as we let him, and invariably one or two of the little peeps will march right up and touch beaks with him. He curls up — to the degree than anything that weighs 90 pounds can curl — next to the brooder and would stay there all night if we would let him.

If we (and by we I mean Beth) get up in the middle of the night to make sure the chicks are doing OK, he'll tag along. And on return, he'll whine at the door, begging to go back.

By breeding, bouviers are supposed to herd cattle and pull milk carts. There's nothing in the manual that says anything about chicken farmer.

Of course there's nothing about being the Guardian of Solid Waste, either. I guess each dog learns his own way. And any diversion that will keep him away from my fruit trees can't be all bad.

Watching My Alpacas Get a Haircut Was Sheer Madness

Six months ago, when I first wrote about our alpaca acquisition, I received a nice note from Sue Hull of Clear Spring, welcoming me into the alpaca fold and asking if we had a shearer lined up to cut their fleece in the spring.

I was happy to be able to provide her with an answer: I told her I didn't know.

Through the course of the year, alpacas grow thick, luxurious layers of fleece, and as this happens, they rather look like a balloon that is very slowly inflating. At some point, something has to be done about this, or each alpaca would take up about 1 square acre of space.

Also, this coat is not terribly comfortable in the summer for a creature used to the high altitudes and cooler temperatures of the Andes. Sue was kind enough to put us on her shearing list, and on April 16, she and two veteran shearers, Christopher and Ramon, arrived to do the deed.

Since the day before was tax day, I felt the date was meaningful, as we would be getting fleeced two days in a row. (For the record, the people at home are getting Very Tired of this joke, but in my opinion, it's timeless).

I don't know what my preconceived notion of an alpaca shearing was, exactly. I guess I assumed it would be like any visit to the beauty shop — the alpaca would stand there while the stylist snipped casually away, and the two of them would gossip about whose children had been expelled from school for sniffing magic markers.

But whatever I had in mind, this wasn't it. Christopher, the shearer, and Ramon, the headsman, asked us to bring in the most difficult animal first. That would be Basilio, a nut-brown elf of an alpaca who kind of has short-man's syndrome — if they wanted difficult, we had difficult.

But the animal was no match for this team, which with well-choreographed quickness, hog-tied him, stretched him out on a mat and fired up the electric clippers. The headsman spins the alpaca, almost as if it were on a spit, so all sides can be quickly shorn. And it's in the headsman's interest to do it right, since for every mistake, Christopher — who shears up to 100 alpacas a day — demands a six-pack of beer in payment. (A shy, retreating type who really needs to come out of his shell, Christopher tosses jolly, good-natured insults to his co-workers' faces, but when their backs are turned, he speaks of them in glowing, appreciative terms. I found this interesting, since it is backward from the way most people behave.)

While this was taking place, Beth gave him a shot (Basilio, not Christopher), Sue did his nails and I stood around with a mild discomfort at being so useless. I felt like I ought to be giving him a mudpack or something. Basilio, meanwhile, contributed to the exercise by shrieking his lungs out.

Christopher is an artist, and Basilio left the procedure looking elegant, with stylish tufts of longer fur left on his legs and forehead. But when he got back into the holding pen, the rest of the boys acted as if they were in middle school — razzing him about his new haircut, kicking, punching, spitting and being truly sociable.

Only when they woke up to the fact that they would be next did they settle down. The other three were more stoic about their trimmings and, frankly, far less entertaining. They are older and know the drill.

And now I do, too. Next year, I'll be ready with the mudpack.

It Takes a Village to Raise Kids

There's a new kid in town. Two, actually. And this time it's my fault.

When you hit your 40s, the nostalgia virus is likely to hit. Songs you hated 25 years before start to sound acceptable, and childhood experiences are remembered as positive experiences, whether they were or not.

I had Toggenburg goats when I was a boy, so having a few extra acres to play with allowed me the chance to revisit past dairying experiences. I'll let you know how it works out.

Strangely, Beth did not need to be talked into acquiring two stunningly cute and eminently huggable little doe kids. We got them from Tracy Garns, who has a wonderful family and a fine herd of Toggenburgs. In fact, it was her young daughter, Courtney, who delivered our set, along with a third male member of the fraternity.

When we first went to visit them, they needed names, and I was pretty set on Lucy and Ethel. I thought that was hilarious, but it only brought out unenthusiastically pursed lips from people to whom I floated the idea. The only ally I had was Tracy and Mike's quick-witted son, Mason, who instantly volunteered that the male goat could be named "Little Ricky." What can I say? The boy knows funny.

We settled on Heidi and Hillary (after the climber, not the clamorer) and I could have sworn during the conversation that I heard Tracy say something about "bottle feeding" but chalked it up to some auditory error on my part.

It wasn't. Twice a day now, and for another month, we heat two bottles of milk and watch the little goats gulp them down, tails frantically wagging in lactic ecstasy. It has to be said that one of the reasons I never had real kids was for moments like this.

I have to take the bottle out of the hot water and splash it on my wrist and, sad to say, Beth had to explain to me that it was to test the temperature. I'd seen women do that before, of course, but I never knew why. I assumed it was for luck or something, like how you toss salt over your shoulder. And for the record, there will be no photos, ever, of me bottle feeding a baby goat, just in case you're getting any ideas.

But if I don't want to be the goats' mommy, there are plenty of willing stand-ins on the farm. The bouvier des Flandres named Opie was volunteer No. 1. He seems to think they are puppies with funny ears.

Copperfield, Sterling, Basilio and Nuchero, the alpacas, meanwhile, say no, no, no. These are baby alpacas with funny ears, and they all want to be the pappy.

And obviously, the goats Pete and Eddy know the truth, so they have staked their claim. Just as obviously, Juliet the cat couldn't care less, although she might take greater interest when they start giving milk.

But the winners in the Toggenburg sweepstakes are the donkeys Becky and Nelson, who believe them to be little donkeys with — well, no donkey is in a position to criticize another's ears.

Every morning, we awake to find them standing with their noses pressed up against the goat barn, waiting for us to open the door. For the balance of the day, the donkeys seldom leave their side.

To this, I have told the donkeys, "Fine. They're yours. Here's the bottle."

Cabbage Best Used a Dog Toy

Rough guess, I would say that we've spent $200 on toys for the bouvier de Flandres named Opie. Off the top of my head, I recall the $18 croaking frog we call Ribbit, the $13 squeaking hedgehog, the $15 Mr. Squirrel and a $17 Mr. Beaver. And that's not to mention various assorted balls and bones and chews. So what are his favorite toys?

In no particular order, they are a limb from a cedar tree, a plastic snow shovel handle, a chunk of a broken ceramic lawn ornament and a cabbage.

I believe there is a teenager correlation here. You buy them a wardrobe of expensive clothes and they insist on wearing the same ratty jeans for 297 consecutive days.

To be fair to the animal, he will every so often play with a store-bought toy. Part of his morning ritual is to grab an "indoor toy" and try to take it outside. We always take it from him before he goes out and he knows we will take it from him, but it doesn't matter. It's like his morning cup of coffee — he needs it to get the mischievous juices flowing.

Once he stuffed both Mr. Squirrel and Mr. Beaver into his mouth, and when I said "drop it" he dutifully dropped Mr. Squirrel. I didn't notice he still had Mr. Beaver until he was outside, where he proceeded to shake it at me, toss his head and laugh his fool ears off.

But given his druthers, he'd rather play with a toy of his own creation. The stick I can understand. All dogs play with sticks. And I sort of get the snow shovel handle — a relic of bygone times that he dug up while I was tilling a new raspberry bed. It's plastic, kind of chewy, very dirty, not atypical of something a dog would be interested in.

But we did raise our eyebrows when we noticed Opie carrying around a chunk of pottery that used to be a frog/rain gauge. I had told Beth that this frog had succumbed to the natural freezing and thawing, expansion and contraction paradigm that is common in nature. But in truth, I had hit it with the lawn mower.

Fearing sharp edges, we quietly removed this object from Opie's field of play when he wasn't looking.

So, obviously, he needed a replacement. I just never thought that he would turn to the compost heap as an impromptu toy store.

Some weeks, or perhaps months, ago, I had purchased a cabbage at the grocery store. I don't remember why; it seemed like a good idea at the time. It sat in the refrigerator for some time, outliving at least two light bulbs. It was one of those situations where each morning we would say, "You know, we really ought to eat that cabbage tonight," but each evening we would manage to find something more palatable, which wasn't too difficult when it comes right down to it.

Time passed. You know you've crossed the line when you stop saying "we really need to eat that cabbage" and start saying "we really need to do something about that cabbage." The tipping point came when we began buying goat's milk four gallons at a time to feed to the baby kids. Something had to go and even though, as a grandchild of the Depression, I hated to waste the 89 cents, out to the compost pile it went.

Forty-five seconds later it was back. By this time, it was bleached white, and Beth about had a heart attack, thinking Opie was toting around a skull. I was instructed to take it from him, but he's big on chewing, so by that time we didn't have a cabbage, we had slaw. I didn't care — 89 cents sure beats $18.

Sociable Swine is a Role Model

Some months ago, I got an e-mail from Katherine McCormick of Smithsburg asking if I wanted a pig.

In these days of uber-spam, I am no stranger to unusual pitches, but although I had been offered everything from home equity lines to methods for increasing the size of my ears, I had never been given the opportunity to obtain a pig.

Katherine noted that this was unusual pig, and hence I suppose she calculated it was in need of an unusual owner. First, it was something of a runt, about half the size of a market porker. Second, it was a very self-confident and inquisitive fellow, with a taste for exploration. So her dad Dave gave him the name of Magellan.

Katherine is headed off to veterinary school at Purdue, so she needed to find a home for Magellan, and since I had — although I don't remember doing this — mentioned something about having some rather curious livestock, she reckoned he might be a good addition.

I wrote back and told her I had to ask Beth — although this was not entirely true. I can picture the average home, where the husband walks in the door with a red, grunting, 150-pound hog in tow and shouts, "Surprise!" In some cases, I can imagine that the wife's reaction would not be 100 percent positive.

It may be only a small exaggeration to say that Beth's reaction would be to tell the pig, "Hi handsome," and go to the kitchen to put on a pot of slop.

Needless to say, she enthusiastically agreed to the acquisition and I set about building a pig residence — which frankly, given my carpentry skills, looks as if it were designed by Picasso, although not as symmetrical — and wiring a fence.

Last Sunday, Katherine, her mom Kendra and Whitey made the delivery. We took a shine to Magellan instantly.

You might think such an animal would have something of an inferiority complex, what with all the filth-and-slob stereotypes hanging around their heads, but Magellan is very comfortable with his pigness.

True to his name, he began to explore his new digs, rooted himself out a mud hole, ate some lunch, stuck his head entirely into his water bucket and then curled up and went to sleep.

By this time, of course, the bouvier des Flandres named Opie was on about his fourth heart attack, leaping and hyperventilating on the other side of the fence. Magellan paid him no mind. The two have since become fast friends — Magellan appreciates Opie's attitude and Opie appreciates Magellan's fragrance.

Contrary to popular thought, the pig is not a dirty creature. There are only three parts of hiis paddock that are a filthy mess:

1. Where he eats.
2. Where he drinks.
3. Where he sleeps.

The rest of the lot is pristine. He is a likable creature, and comes running whenever we pay him a visit. We sit in his lot and he nuzzles us all over with his muddy snout, nibbles our shoulders, grunts, slobbers and is truly sociable.

Even Hannah the bulldog, who is normally Very Suspicious of any new critter we happen to haul in has become his pal.

Truth be told, the pig is much like a dog himself. Except, I told Opie, he doesn't chase cars, he doesn't stare off at the church on Sunday and bark at the Christians, he doesn't torture the UPS drivers and he doesn't go full freakout every time a Canada goose flies overhead.

We knew we were getting a pig; we did not know we were getting a role model.

To be continued...